MW00488831

RECLAIMING
REVIVAL

Victoria Buckslot
(678)925-3391

desire
humility
consistency
(faith)

RECLAIMING
REVIVAL

CALLING A GENERATION TO
CONTEND FOR HISTORIC AWAKENING

COREY RUSSELL
& BILLY HUMPHREY

© Copyright 2022–Corey Russell and Billy Humphrey

All rights reserved. This book is protected by the copyright laws of the United States of America. This book may not be copied or reprinted for commercial gain or profit. The use of short quotations or occasional page copying for personal or group study is permitted and encouraged. Permission will be granted upon request. Unless otherwise identified, Scripture quotations are taken from the New King James Version. Copyright © 1982 by Thomas Nelson, Inc. Used by permission. All rights reserved. All emphasis within Scripture quotations is the author's own. Please note that Destiny Image's publishing style capitalizes certain pronouns in Scripture that refer to the Father, Son, and Holy Spirit, and may differ from some publishers' styles. Take note that the name satan and related names are not capitalized. We choose not to acknowledge him, even to the point of violating grammatical rules.

DESTINY IMAGE® PUBLISHERS, INC.

P.O. Box 310, Shippensburg, PA 17257-0310

"Promoting Inspired Lives."

This book and all other Destiny Image and Destiny Image Fiction books are available at Christian bookstores and distributors worldwide.

For more information on foreign distributors, call 717-532-3040.

Reach us on the Internet: www.destinyimage.com.

ISBN 13 TP: 978-0-7684-6090-2
ISBN 13 eBook: 978-0-7684-6091-9
ISBN 13 HC: 978-0-7684-6093-3
ISBN 13 LP: 978-0-7684-6092-6

For Worldwide Distribution, Printed in the U.S.A.
1 2 3 4 5 6 7 8 / 26 25 24 23 22

We dedicate this book to intercessors all over the earth who are believing for revival.

ACKNOWLEDGMENTS

We are very grateful to those intercessors and revivalists who have gone before us. They and their stories have served as catalysts to our hunger and desire for historic awakening. We thank God for their lives and examples.

We would like to thank Edie Mourey for co-laboring with us in bringing forth the message in this book.

We want to acknowledge and thank the team at Destiny Image. We are grateful for your dedication to producing quality books that promote living Spirit-inspired and Spirit-empowered lives. We want to especially thank Larry Sparks for his partnership and for seeing the importance of calling a generation to contend for awakening.

CONTENTS

FOREWORD

The Church of America must experience a fresh, mighty wave of revival—or else. It is simply non-negotiable. As Billy Humphrey and Corey Russell write in the very last words of this book, "Revival and nothing less. Revival or we never rest. Revival now, oh God, we cry. Revival now or we will die!"

They are not exaggerating in the least. It really is a matter of revival or we die.

That's because America is at a tipping point, being torn apart at the seams and convulsing deeply in moral and spiritual confusion. But that's because the Church of America has failed to shine the light, failed to demonstrate the reality of the gospel, failed to show the world a better way. In fact, for a full generation now, rather than the Church changing the world, the world has changed the Church. How can this be?

1

In so many ways, as American followers of Jesus, we are known for our divisions, for our sexual and financial scandals, for our hypocrisy, for our political obsessions—really, for everything *but* our relationship with Jesus. Something is terribly wrong.

The good news is that God Himself longs to pour out His Spirit afresh, and for several decades now, a cry to Heaven has been rising 24/7—a cry for revival, for outpouring, for awakening. The Lord will respond to our cries!

But what, exactly, is revival? In this powerful and stirring book, Billy and Corey paint a picture of revival that you can not only see but that you can feel and even taste. Their words, which will convict and challenge, remind us of the power of divine encounter, of the reality of the Spirit's visitation, of the transformational character of a true move of God. And as you read, your own heart will burn, "Lord, won't You do it again? And won't You start with me?"

As the authors share their own journeys, with humility and honesty, and as they describe the mighty works of God from revivals in the past, you will experience a hunger and thirst rising in your own heart. Grab hold of that hunger and let it drive you afresh to pray, to fast, to turn away from sin, to share your faith boldly. And then make a determination: No matter how long it takes and no matter how many obstacles I have to overcome, I must experience God for myself in a deeper, more powerful way. I must experience revival!

That's the hunger that the Lord is looking for, and that is the hunger to which He will respond. In fact, it is the degree of your spiritual hunger that will determine your capacity to be visited by the Lord. He pours out His Spirit on the thirsty land. How thirsty are you?

It is my prayer that, once you finish this timely book, revival will become non-negotiable for you as well. With it, all things are possible. In fact, America's greatest days could be ahead. Without it, we are in dire trouble.

What, then, will it be? I say, "Send a fresh wave of revival, Lord, and start the work here and now in me!"

Dr. Michael L. Brown
Host of the *Line of Fire* radio broadcast
Author of *Revival Or We Die:*
A Great Awakening Is Our Only Hope

INTRODUCTION

The whole globe is in transition.

> *For we know that the whole creation groans and labors with birth pangs together until now. Not only that, but we also who have the firstfruits of the Spirit, even we ourselves groan within ourselves, eagerly waiting for the adoption, the redemption of our body.* (Romans 8:22–23)

Creation is longing and groaning for redemption from the bondage of sin that has weighed it down. This groan is in the sky, on the earth, and rumbling through society. All creation is groaning. This groan is manifesting through the historic rise of pestilences, earthquakes, hurricanes, and tornadoes.

Not only is creation itself groaning, but there is a groan deep within us all—a longing to throw off this body of death and be fully absorbed in God. The Spirit is groaning within us, making intercession with Jesus for the full will of God to come about in our lives.

> *Likewise the Spirit also helps in our weaknesses.*
> *For we do not know what we should pray for as*
> *we ought, but the Spirit Himself makes interces-*
> *sion for us with groanings which cannot be uttered.*
> (Romans 8:26)

WHAT IS THIS GROAN?

We believe it's the deep cry within every one of us to fully experience everything that God intended in the beginning. Think back to the garden, where God and man walked in seamless intimacy, in unbroken connection. And out of the overflow of this connection, man was commissioned to rightly take dominion over the earth.

Sadly, in many places the current state of the Church is disconnected from this intimacy and our Heaven-breathed calling for dominion. From the pain of this dispossession, the groan and vision for revival have begun to awaken in the heart of a people longing for more. Where we have chosen to anesthetize our souls with a thousand lesser comforts and settle down into a world we were meant to be passing through, we must now honestly come to grips with the reality of our state.

We are desperately in need of reclaiming what we have lost: namely, an outpouring of the Holy Spirit upon the

Church that awakens her from her sleep and causes her to walk in the glory and the fear of God to the extent that entire cities, regions, and nations are impacted by a pure confrontation of God. This groan over our desperate state is calling us to reclaim revival.

WHAT IS REVIVAL?

Revival is a divine season where God openly manifests the rule and reign of His Son by the outpouring of the Holy Spirit and the release of apostolic preaching. It's a snapshot of the coming day when the heavens are rent and God comes down, dismantling the powers of darkness and loosing satan's hold over the earth.

Revival drives men, women, and children back to God. Revival is Heaven's onslaught against every system and structure that have been set up in opposition to Jesus. It stirs up a deep longing for the manifest presence of God. Ultimately, revival generates a cry in us all for the return of our Lord Jesus Christ.

In days of revival, God gives us a glimpse of that coming day when Heaven and Earth are fully one and man and God walk in seamless intimacy once again—where the whole creation is brought fully into divine order.

Beginning with the day of Pentecost, there have been seasons in time where God stepped down and revived that which was lost in His people. Every one of these historic seasons was preceded by a breakdown in the culture and in the Church. And now we find ourselves in a similar season.

In these days, we have witnessed more Christian leaders publicly turn from their faith than any other time in our lives. Ministry failures are at an epidemic proportion. We don't say this to judge but to tremble and groan. Culture has continued to boil with perversion and sin, and the outcome is many churches and leaders are now influenced by the culture more than they are by the eternal truths of the Word of God. The frog is in the kettle, and the water is beginning to churn.

We believe that Jesus' indictment and invitation to the Laodicean church in Revelation 3 is beckoning to us in these days:

> *I know your works, that you are neither cold nor hot. I could wish you were cold or hot. So then, because you are lukewarm, and neither cold nor hot, I will vomit you out of My mouth. Because you say, "I am rich, have become wealthy, and have need of nothing"—and do not know that you are wretched, miserable, poor, blind, and naked—I counsel you to buy from Me gold refined in the fire, that you may be rich; and white garments, that you may be clothed, that the shame of your nakedness may not be revealed; and anoint your eyes with eye salve, that you may see. As many as I love, I rebuke and chasten. Therefore be zealous and repent. Behold, I stand at the door and knock. If anyone hears my voice and opens the door, I will come into him and dine with him, and he with Me.* (Revelation 3:15–20)

Our journey to revival begins with the painful recognition of how far we have fallen and how out of touch with reality we truly are. The main thing that strikes us in this passage is how we assess ourselves versus how Jesus does. Our assessment can be drastically different from His, yet we do not know it. That deeply troubles us because we have been guilty of comparing ourselves with others in dedication to God, imagining that we somehow are doing well because of our own measuring stick. When we fall into the deception of comparing ourselves with others, we end up leaning back into self-confidence instead of leaning into dependence on Him. This is the essence of lukewarmness—believing we have no need and all the while we can't see the shocking state of our own spiritual blindness and poverty.

Jesus is knocking at the door of the Church in this hour, disturbing the machine that has us believing we're safe because we're prosperous. His knock is disturbing our lives, our ministries, our callings, and tenderly yet firmly reiterating the same thing, "Church in America, I want greater intimacy with you. I want greater access to you. I want to dine with you. I want to be closer to you. I want to come in to you!"

Friends, know this: He won't relent until we finally give up on our ways and open the door to let Him in.

This book is a call from two men who have been limping through the painful recognition of how disconnected we are from Jesus, from two men who have found that the groan for eternity has been quieted by all the stuff of our culture. We aren't men who have figured anything out, but we have heard

His call to open up and let Him in, and we want to awaken as many as God will allow to this same hunger and desire.

In 2020, we started a podcast titled *Gripped*. It was born out of the desire to shake ourselves and awaken the Church. We wanted to share with anyone who would listen what has so gripped us during personal and corporate times of revival, as well as what we've learned from our studies of biblical and historical revivals. We were blown away with the response that so many had to that first season. We literally got testimonies from around the world of people who were longing and aching for a God-birthed, God-breathed outpouring of the Holy Spirit. Many testified how the podcast had reignited a vision and passion for revival in their hearts once again.

After some time in prayer, we felt from the Lord that we were to take the content from that original season and expand upon it in book form to pierce hearts with the very ache that has so inexhaustibly possessed us. Using a similar format as we did in the podcast, both of us contribute to the discussions presented in the following chapters with the hope that the burden the Lord has put upon us for a Heaven-sent "inbreaking" of holy power will be imparted to you.

We want you to read these pages with an open and vulnerable heart, ready to hear what the Spirit is speaking to you, how He may be calling you to consider your ways, and what changes He may want you to make. We all only get one go-round in this life. We believe this book is yet another alarm calling us to awaken to Him because the hour is urgent. Will you seek Him while He may be found? Will you turn from every doubtful thing and embrace Him fully? Once and for all, will you open your heart and let Him in?

MARKED BY REVIVAL FOR REVIVAL

We first met in Kansas City, Missouri, in 2003 at the International House of Prayer (IHOPKC). From the very beginning, we recognized we both shared a deep hunger for God. We saw and respected in each other an intense desire for greater intimacy with Jesus and a desperate longing for more revelation of Him. To this day, whenever we get together, it's explosive!

Billy: I remember showing up in Kansas City and thinking, *These are the prayer people. These are the intercession and revival people.* But when I got around the prayer room, I thought it was a bit calm and subdued compared to what I'd seen in other revivals and even in my own youth ministry back home, where we had experienced an outpouring of the Holy Spirit. I remember one day looking across the room during a prayer meeting at IHOPKC and seeing Corey, this twenty-six-year-old dude with his intense face. He was pacing and praying like a wild man. Immediately, I wanted to meet him.

The first time we decided to connect was at McDonald's. As we were sharing our hearts and our hunger for God, the power of God hit us right there in McDonald's. It was intense! We were literally jerking and shaking under the power of God right there in the restaurant.

A few weeks later, I happened to be sitting next to Corey's wife, Dana, listening to Corey preach. I asked her, "He's up there shaking and all. Does he do that all the time?"

"No," Dana said. "That started when he met you."

Corey: Yes, that's what happened. I believe it's the Spirit of God in me resonating with the Spirit of God in Billy. Whenever we have the opportunity to minister together, there always seems to be the kiss of the Lord on it.

Billy: I think Corey and I have a shared marking by the Spirit of the Lord. There is that depth of desire and hunger for an outbreak of the Holy Spirit. Neither of us want to have a "nice meeting" as we minister to people. We want the full takeover of the Holy Spirit in our churches, in our ministries, and in society—where Jesus takes hold of us all and manifests the Glory of His Kingdom.

Corey and I share a vision for something far beyond what we have ever seen with our physical eyes. Once we begin to touch it a little bit, once the Spirit of God begins to break in a little bit, there's that thing inside both of us that begins to witness to us, "There's so much more!" I believe this marking is not only for Corey and me. There are others. Maybe you are one of those and what you're reading in this book is resonating in your spirit, too. Perhaps you're sensing church as usual is done. 2020 has taught us that. God is changing the way that the Church is going to be expressed and understood. I believe God wants to mark you, too! That you would not be satisfied until you experience a complete God-breathed takeover of the Holy Spirit. I'm asking Him to mark you now.

Corey and I have been marked by revival for revival, and that's what ignites when we come together in prayer and fasting, intercession and worship, preaching and teaching, or sharing and fellowshipping.

Corey: I would say that I was marked for revival in my salvation and the season that immediately ensued. On February 18, 1997, on a Tuesday at noon in a college parking lot, I got out of a van, fell to my knees, and cried at the top of my lungs, *"Jesus, I give You my life. I'm Yours!"* The fifteen minutes prior were characterized by a power encounter with the Holy Spirit, where He came into the van, causing me to manifest demons that were choking me and trying with all their power to keep me from saying the name, "Jesus." But after several tries, I took a deep breath, and with all the power inside me, I screamed His name. In my salvation, I witnessed the effortlessness of the power of God that can save a soul, break the power of the demonic, and deliver a drug addict all in one moment. This is what revival is to me. It's when Jesus flexes His superior power over all the works of the devil. Over the next six months, I would see this reality demonstrated time and time again as He did it to my friends and my brother and as we continued to see a sweeping move of God that impacted our city in a dramatic way.

There was no place off-limits to the presence of God. He moved at the revival meetings, in my bedroom, in my car, at my college, at the gas station, and in the grocery store. God's presence broke out everywhere, and His presence was perceptible to everyone, even unbelievers. He shook our local high school. He shook our city. He shook the church. He saved many, delivered many, brought the backslidden back, restored marriages, healed bodies, and much more. I remember witnessing people getting instantly baptized in the Holy Spirit with no altar call or any instruction, and many of these people were from denominations that didn't believe in the baptism of the Holy Spirit.

All these realities were amazing, but as I think back on that season, the prayer meetings were what marked me the most. The spirit of intercession rested heavily on us for hours before services. Furthermore, I saw how God uses travailing prayer to birth fresh releases of the Spirit. It was in that season when I spent the majority of time with these older women who were intercessors. They taught me how to pray and to move with the Spirit in prayer in a season of revival.

Twenty-five years later, the depth of that first season has ruined me for anything less.

Billy: As a youth pastor in 1995, I was touched by the Brownsville revival, named for the Brownsville Assembly of God Church in Pensacola, Florida. Steve Hill was the evangelist that the Lord used mightily there. But what stood out to me was how the presence and power of God rested on "regular" people, not just the platform ministers. The members of the prayer team would reach out with one finger on someone's forehead, saying, "Fire!" And the person getting prayed for would get hit with the power of God. It looked as if the person receiving prayer was getting hit with a baseball bat.

I remember my first trip to Brownsville with some of our church staff—the senior pastor and other pastoral staff—some of whom were a bit skeptical about what they had heard about the meetings. But I'll never forget when we arrived at the church campus. There was a line of about fifteen hundred people at noon, and the meeting didn't start until seven in the evening. I had seen people camp out for concerts, or the newest ride at amusement parks, but church? I had never seen that before.

The meeting finally started, and we were inside. The worship was intense and powerful. And after the preaching, an altar call was given. People didn't walk slowly to the front—they ran! I could see their faces and hear them crying out. They were gripped by conviction. They were broken and wailing.

Later during the ministry time, I saw this petite older lady come over to my pastor. She was on their ministry team. My pastor was a godly man, a stable guy, not given to excess or hype. As this little lady laid her hands on my pastor, he went crashing down. *Crack!* The back of his head bluntly hit the wooden pew behind him. I thought we would have to call the paramedics.

As I crouched down to look at him, he was out of it. I didn't know what to do. I stayed with him for several minutes until he started coming around.

"Are you okay?" I asked.

"Yeah. That's powerful. I feel the Lord," he said.

"You hit your head harder than I've ever—I mean—I thought you were completely knocked out!"

"Oh, I didn't hit my head," he told me. But I knew what I saw. I had seen and heard the sound of him hitting his head as he fell like a dead man. I had watched him get "slain in the Spirit," smacking his head in the process, yet he assured me as he got up that he didn't feel a thing!

That experience with my pastor going down under the power of God radically changed my understanding of God. Up until that evening, I had never seen God's power unleashed in that way. My limited knowledge of His power got blown up that night. The roof of my vision of who God was came off, as I realized, with God, anything can happen. He is Almighty God. He is all-powerful!

Corey: That's a great story, but I think my favorite one of Billy's experiences at Brownsville was when Dr. Michael Brown prayed for him and his friend Ryan.

Billy: Dr. Brown is a good friend of mine today. Back then I only knew Him as Michael Brown the teacher at the Brownsville Revival. My friend Ryan and I were in a meeting one time, and we were specifically wanting Dr. Brown to pray for us. He was at the entrance of the sanctuary and walking out into the lobby area, laying hands on people who were gathering around him. The lobby and sanctuary were crowded with hundreds of people. Yet we could see Dr. Brown laying hands on people, and they were flying into the air—I'm talking two or three feet—as if they were being thrown.

Ryan and I saw Dr. Brown coming our way. We knew it wasn't about the man but about how the Lord was using Dr. Brown to touch people with His power. Dr. Brown was just a conduit. People around us were getting delivered, healed, touched, and changed as God's power was breaking out in the building.

We were desperate for God's presence, but as Dr. Brown got closer to us, the presence of God was increasing to a level that began to strike a bit of holy fear in us. It was getting intense. Between that and the bodies flying as he neared us, the fear of the Lord began to radically intensify. I thought, *Oh no, what did I get myself into?* God's presence was bearing down on us. The air was heavy. The Lord was moving in like a massive giant lumbering our way. A collision felt inevitable.

Then *pow!* As Dr. Brown put one finger on Ryan, the Spirit hit him, like he had been shot with a gun. Ryan fell back several feet shouting, "Ohhhh!!!" And I was thinking, *How do I get out of this?*

Next thing I knew, Dr. Brown had his hand on my head and said, "Fire!" Into the air I went—up and back—until *bang!* I hit the ground.

I finally came to sometime later. I looked up and realized I was ten to fifteen feet away from where I had been when Dr. Brown had first laid his finger on me. Sitting there, I tried to make sense of what had just happened to me. I felt something like an electrical current shooting through me and coursing all over my body. I realized in that moment that God was much more powerful, much more present, much more available than I had ever known before.

Here's the point: When God makes Himself known, there is no question about it. And when He touches our hearts in a dynamic way during revival, He marks us. He expands our vision to see something transcendent, something beyond human ability expressed. We see Him. We see His power and glory. And we are wrecked for being satisfied with anything less.

2

JESUS AT THE CENTER

When God comes, *God comes*. Think about what that means. God coming to you, your church, your city. What would that look like? When Heaven invades Earth, unimaginable things happen. The Scriptures bear that out. When God comes, the earth quakes, the skies resound with thunder and lightning, the seas roar, and nations tremble.

The Old Testament prophets spoke about God coming to execute righteousness and to measure out judgment. Malachi spoke of God "suddenly" coming to His temple. And he said that, when God came, He would come *"like a refiner's fire and like launderers' soap"* (Mal. 3:2).

Looking at biblical and historical revivals, we understand conviction, travail, judgments, earthquakes, healings, deliverances, and mass salvations—they all come when Jesus invades Earth, time, and space. When Jesus comes, He takes center stage in the hearts and lives of people, in the pulpits of His Church, and in the lifestyles of His priests.

It's in seasons of revival that Jesus becomes first. Jesus becomes precious to His people again, and we become highly sensitive to doing anything, seeing anything, hearing anything, or saying anything that offends Him. It's in revival that the worth and the value of Jesus are restored and we worship Him in a manner He is due.

God sends revival because we need reviving. He sends revival because He wants to restore something we used to have but have lost.

Billy: When God descends on a place, city, region, or nation, look out! The glory of God has increased from being upon an individual to resting upon a corporate people in a broad place or region. When He comes this way, the intensity of what can happen ratchets up exponentially.

I remember what happened, for example, when Corey preached on Malachi 1 in Atlanta in 2005. As Corey was preaching, I was hit with intercession. While he released the words of Malachi 1:10–11, I physically fell from my chair and began wailing in travail:

> *"Who is there even among you who would shut the doors, so that you would not kindle fire on My altar in vain? I have no pleasure in you," says the Lord of hosts, "nor will I accept an offering from your hands. For from the rising of the sun, even to*

its going down, My name shall be great among the
Gentiles; in every place incense shall be offered to
My name, and a pure offering; for My name shall
be great among the nations," says the Lord of hosts.

The anointing that was on Corey in preaching broke out upon the room, and many began to fall out of their chairs and onto the floor in groaning and intercession. All I know is when Corey started to speak about shutting the doors, power hit the place, and I was doubled over on the floor in intercession for the next hour. The room came unglued, lit up with fire.

Corey: Malachi's mission was to call the nation back to God, and it started with the priesthood. They were to serve as God's mediators of blessing and favor on the nation and thereby the nations. In the same way today, the Church is called to be salt and light in a dark and decaying world. Whenever God wants to send revival, it must begin with His people. God must first deal with the state of His people to bring a shift in cities and nations.

In Malachi's day, the priesthood had fallen so far that people were bringing lame, blind, and sick animals as offerings. They were just checking off the box of religious duty, and this was grievous to God.

"A son honors his father, and a servant his master. If
then I am the Father, where is My honor? And if I
am a Master, where is My reverence? says the Lord
of hosts to you priests who despise My name. Yet you
say, 'In what way have we despised Your name?'
You offer defiled food on My altar, but say, 'In what

way have we defiled You?' By saying, 'The table of the Lord is contemptible.' And when you offer the blind as a sacrifice, is it not evil? And when you offer the lame and sick, is it not evil? Offer it then to your governor! Would he be pleased with you? Would he accept you favorably?" says the Lord of hosts. (Malachi 1:6–8)

After Malachi indicted the people over their pathetic offerings, he made one of the most striking and poignant questions that I can hear echoing within the Church in these days:

Who is there even among you who would shut the doors, so that you would not kindle fire on My altar in vain? (Malachi 1:10)

Malachi called the people to shut down the whole sacrificial system because—every time they offered the lame, sick leftovers—they were heaping judgment on themselves and on the nation. Though this sounds really intense to us today, I believe God is saying something like this to the American Church: "Shut down business as usual and restore a pure offering of worship and prayer back to Me!"

We have become way too comfortable checking off our weekly box of attending church while living the other six days and twenty-three hours of the week disconnected from Him, and I can feel the heart of God longing for greater intimacy with His people. I believe that 2020 with the global shutdown was a whisper of this reality from God to the Church, but I'm afraid that we are so earnest about getting the machine running again and us getting back to normal that we aren't hearing what He is saying. That terrifies me because, if 2020 was a whisper, I don't want to know what anything more would sound like.

Billy: That leads us to these questions: Have we not had enough meetings? Have we not done enough worship events? So, why don't we see awakening in our churches? Why don't we see revival in our cities? Could it be we need to look at what we are offering to the Lord—what we are actually giving to God?

Corey: I'm convinced that we've backslidden to a convenience-driven, man-centered form of Christianity because we've lost revelation of God's worth. I believe preaching and worship songs that put the eyes of the Church back on Him are going to restore a pure devotion worthy of His glory. We've become way too familiar with Him, and we desperately need to revere and tremble at the holiness and awesomeness of God.

Billy: Today, we must ask ourselves this: Have we been doing church in a way that's more for man than it is for God? Have we been doing church in a way that "scratches" our religious "itch" but doesn't call to the depth of our Heavenly Father?

We have made the Church and our meetings all about us. Is the padding on the seats thick enough? Is the air conditioner cold enough? Are the colors in the lobby warm and inviting? Is the music too soft, too loud? Have we done everything necessary to make people feel at ease and comfortable?

I think our environments should be welcoming and not an impediment to worship and hearing the preaching of the

,vord, but we *must* put God first. When will Jesus Christ have the preeminence in His own Church? When will He be the center of all we do?

I'm broken over the fact that we have worked very hard to make everyone else comfortable in our meetings while we have made our meetings uncomfortable for the One who should have center stage. Have we truly become so seeker-sensitive that we have become God-insensitive?

If that's the case, we need to look again at Malachi 1:10 and ask ourselves, "Is it time to shut it down?" Perhaps that's what God was doing in 2020 with the pandemic lockdowns. Could God have been releasing a global Malachi 1:10?

Corey: I believe God has been saying, "Shut it down." I believe He is doing that personally as well. For years, we've been saying, "If I had more time, I'd spend more time with God." So, 2020 comes along, and we all quickly find out that the time at home exposed our boredom with God and our lack of a true, living, experiential knowledge of Him. I think the shutdown is a corporate call back to God as well as an individual call back to Him.

> *But you, when you pray, go into your room, and when you have shut your door, pray to your Father who is in the secret place; and your Father who sees in secret will reward you openly.* (Matthew 6:6)

I can feel the heart of the Father longing for "eye contact" with His people. It requires "shutting a door" that enables us to "look at Him." God wants us back into our rooms—back into the secret place. He wants us to shut the door and pray. Pray to the Father. Get to know Him in intimate fellowship and prayer. Shut the door and get rid of the "system" you've used in the past to do what looks "spiritual" yet has no real power.

And it's a kindness of the Lord to tell us to shut it all down, reboot, reconnect, and then reemerge in this season by making Him foremost, primary, chief, and center.

After giving one of the strongest rebukes, Malachi gives us one of the greatest prophecies in Scripture:

> *"For from the rising of the sun even to its going down, My name shall be great among the Gentiles; in every place incense shall be offered to My name, and a pure offering; for My name shall be great among the nations," says the Lord of hosts.* (Malachi 1:11)

God shuts down one thing to open up another, and I believe that we are in the midst of a transition. I believe the days of "Sunday-only Christianity" are over. Jesus did not die for 45 minutes and $20 once a week, but He died for nearness 24/7.

A pure offering is going to be restored to the Church across the earth, and I believe it will be this purity and glory resting on the Church that will provoke Israel to jealousy.

For Malachi to prophesy that the Gentiles would offer incense to God's name was a shocker to Israel. It was a total repudiation of their false religious system. They heard the message loud and clear: "What you have offered Me is repulsive, and I'm actually turning to the Gentiles. That's going to provoke you, but I'm going to bring a worship movement.

Your worship has been abhorrent, but I will raise up a worship movement across the nations that will declare the greatness of My name."

I feel like we are in a global moment where God shut us down. He did this so that we would get rid of our programs, our personalities, our platforms—everything man-made and man-driven. He is after a pure offering from us. He can raise up a global prayer and worship movement that puts His Son at the center. It puts the Man, Christ Jesus, in the highest place.

When we gather together, we must remember that we gather together for Him. He should be our priority, our first thought, our first inclination. And that is the spirit of revival. That is what revival is. We turn away from lesser things, lesser loves and lovers. We turn away from the things that distract us from Jesus. We break away from religious forms of going through the motions of religious acts. And we turn to Jesus with all our heart, soul, mind, and strength.

I want to admonish you that, if there are distractions and attractions in your life that are drawing you away from the simplicity and purity of devotion to Jesus, stop! Stop right now! He stopped the world in 2020 to bring us back to Himself. And if the pandemic hasn't worked that into us all by now, I promise He is jealous enough to create more contexts that will shut us down from offering Him less than what He is worthy of, which is our wholehearted devotion.

I love what Martyn Lloyd-Jones said about revival—that it's the mass glorification of Jesus Christ.

Billy: That's right. We need Jesus repositioned at the center. We want to adore Him as the chief cause and aim of the Church. We want Him glorified and exalted in all we do. We need our hearts gripped with a vision to love Him with everything that's in us.

When Jesus takes center stage once again in our hearts and our churches, that's revival.

3

TIMES OF REFRESHING

When we talk about revival, we're talking about Jesus. After all, He is the One we want. He is the One we long for, and He is the One who longs for us. The longing and the eager hope we have within us have been stirred by His Spirit resident within us. It's God in us calling to God. It's the Spirit saying, "Come," and then we as the Bride begin to cry out the same.

We must remember God is the One initiating it all. He is the One who causes our deep to call out to Him. He then comes to us in response to this mutual, deep longing.

Corey: Ultimately, revival involves friendship with God. We touch His pain and His longing through the Holy Spirit who dwells in us. I think understanding this has helped me to frame revival.

We can make revival all about the meetings, especially what is transpiring in the meetings. And we're grateful for that. We want to encounter God in powerful ways as we gather together unto Him. That's good, but there's more.

We actually want to build a place for Him to inhabit or dwell. He is longing to dwell on the earth with us. As intercessors, we want to get awakened to this groan for Him as friends that steward the gap and the journey for years and decades between those moments where He comes close and those times He seems to pull back.

God comes close to His people, and it cuts us. Yet it also answers our desire for His tangible presence, so we're wrecked for anything less than that. And then He pulls back, and this is where we must persevere in hope. This is where we must sustain the groan in intimacy with Him.

Peter said in Acts 3:19,

> *Repent therefore and be converted, that your sins may be blotted out, so that times of refreshing may come from the presence of the Lord.*

There are divine seasons where God openly manifests the rule and the reign of His Son by the outpouring of the Holy Spirit and the release of apostolic preaching. This is our working definition for revival. It's those divine seasons when the Father makes it known to everyone that Jesus is exalted at His right hand. In times like these, the Spirit brings conviction of sin. People begin to experience the outpouring of the Holy Spirit, and the Word of God goes forth, wreaking havoc against the kingdom of darkness.

Billy: When Peter mentioned "times of refreshing," he was speaking about an appointed time—a *kairos* moment. I like to think of it as a moment that God has on His calendar. He's identified these times, these moments in history, where He says, "I'm going to change the normal order by opening the veil, pulling back the curtains, and releasing a manifestation of My Kingdom in an outwardly, overt way so that all flesh recognizes Heaven is now on display." Of course, if Heaven is on display, the King is the centerpiece of that.

These times of refreshing are a portent. They're a foretelling, then, of the day when Jesus Christ rules and reigns in the earth. Revival foreshadows the day when *"the earth will be filled with the knowledge of the glory of the Lord as the waters cover the sea"* (Hab. 2:14). So, revival is a prophetic sign of what's to come.

Generations get to experience these moments of the glory of the Lord manifesting upon the earth. Such times are hallmarked by deep conviction of sin. Don't tell me revival is happening if people are still living in compromise. If people are still lying, cheating, mistreating each other, viewing pornography on the side, and acting pridefully, don't try to say revival is happening. No, revival brings a fire—an all-consuming fire—that burns up all of that.

Look at Acts 5:1–11; when you see the glory that was upon the New Testament church in that day, they couldn't bring sin in the glory zone. Ananias and Sapphira tried to, and they died as a result. As the glory increases, sin gets judged in a greater measure.

Corey: Exactly, because God is closer during revivals.

Billy: When God comes down in revival, our hearts are judged, and conviction grows in intensity. We see people who were "fine" before the revival hit suddenly confessing hidden issues and sins.

I remember when an awakening hit IHOPKC and the House of Prayer in Atlanta in 2010. More sin was confessed in that first month than the entire previous year. It moved backsliders to the front of the sanctuary and down on their knees at the altars. It caused those who were unsaved to have an awareness of sin. Sinners were getting saved at the same time that church members were confessing compromise and sin. The Church was getting right with God!

We must look back at the term used for *times of refreshing* in the Greek. It's *anapsucho*, which means a recovery of breath. Imagine something that was dormant or dead, and then the winds of God come back into it, making it alive and animate once again. That's revival, and that's what happens to the Church. Those who are dead come alive. And these times of refreshing are appointed times for the recovery of breath until the coming of the Lord.

Corey: I think about John 16:8–11, where Jesus said,

> *And when He has come, He will convict the world of sin, and of righteousness, and of judgment: of sin, because they do not believe in Me; of righteousness, because I go to My Father and you see Me no more; of judgment, because the ruler of this world is judged.*

Jesus was saying there are three realities the world experiences when He sends the Holy Spirit. The Holy Spirit convicts the world of (1) sin, (2) righteousness, and (3) judgment. These realities are highlighted in seasons of revival. The Holy Spirit does this work all the time in the world; however, it is increased a hundredfold during times of refreshing. And that's why Peter in Acts 3:19 admonished the crowd around him to repent and be converted.

4

LIFTING THE BAR

In chapter one, we addressed some wrong ideas we have about revival. We discussed how people speak of revival as if it were simply special meetings that churches have over the course of a few days or a week. Thus far, we've endeavored to rectify some misconceptions about what revival is and what it's not, but there's another important clarification we want to make. The size, scope, or reach of Holy Spirit activities must be considered as well.

The sphere of impact matters when it comes to identifying a revival because it reveals the scope or reach of God's move upon people. A few people being saved or baptized does not a revival make. And when it comes to a personal renewal of sorts, we want to be careful in how we choose to categorize or identify such an experience. Yes, we may be experiencing a personal revival, or yes, a local assembly may be enjoying a fresh outpouring of the Spirit in their midst, but it's not the same in scope as a regional revival or the global outpouring like the one God has promised His people before He wraps up this age.

Billy: There are even those who assert, "We are revival right now." They may be pointing to carrying the Holy Spirit in their lives since He moves within them and thereby affects their surroundings. And in a sense, they are correct. The eternal truth is we carry the Holy Spirit within us. He dwells inside us, and we can literally fellowship with Him 24/7. The Holy Spirit is far more available to us than what any of us are tapping into. It's important, however, to rightly differentiate between being carriers of the Holy Spirit and having an authentic, God-breathed revival.

Other times when people speak of revival, they are referring to a series of good meetings where there are a few words of knowledge, a couple of people being healed, and several individuals being saved. And they say, "Revival is happening." And the problem I have with this is it takes the concept of the recovery of breath and awakening *in the earth* and diminishes it to the few words of knowledge, a couple of people healed, and several individuals saved. I'm not against these things happening. I celebrate them, and we should all celebrate them, but my point is that these are all things that should be part of *normal* Christianity. What I tend to think is we've lowered the bar so far on what Christianity is supposed to look like that it's caused us to lower the bar on what revival looks like.

A dozen people getting saved and baptized in the Holy Spirit is awesome! But let's get honest and recognize there is so much more available! A much greater impact is possible. There is an onslaught of the Holy Spirit that will bring an entire region under the authority and the glory of the Kingdom of God. For years now in our church in Atlanta, we've been praying for a fifty-mile zone of Kingdom influence, a fifty-mile zone of glory, a demon-free reality that is in every store, every bank, every school, every church, and every business. We want to see the fire of God fall in all these places. If the fire of God can fall in a room, it can fall on a city. If it can fall on a heart, it can fall on a region. You see, the size, the scope, and the reach of a true revival is far greater than it being upon only one heart or in one location.

God is not bound by distance. Everything is small to Him. What's twelve feet versus twelve-hundred miles to Him? It's nothing! God can bring an entire region under His glory. That's what we see in historic revivals and great awakenings. When we diminish the definition of revival to a little, positive, Kingdom progress, we are not doing justice to what revival really is. We must lift the bar. We must get a higher vision. We must regain the wonder of what God can do and what revival can be.

We don't want to call a little spark a bonfire. That amounts to hype. When we see what happened in Acts 2, Acts 5, Acts 11–13, and Acts 19, we see these explosions of the glory of God in the earth. We must not take the biblical record of revival and minimize it. When we do, we do violence to the truth of what the Bible promises us regarding God's outpouring in the earth and His movement across the globe.

Corey: I'm truly grateful for a person who is saved, delivered, healed, and restored. I never get over watching God touch a person with His presence and see him cry tears of repentance or of desire to be God's child. But we must make it very clear: A good meeting is not revival. When I think of the scope and disruption that revival brings, I think of Acts 19 and what God did in Ephesus.

Paul was in Ephesus, and in his two years of ministry there, the worship of Diana and the industry behind it were destroyed. This would be equivalent to the power of God hitting Las Vegas and resulting in all the casinos being shut down and the gambling industry there abolished. Billions of dollars would be lost to a city like Vegas because of the impact of the gospel against a sin industry, and that's what happened in Ephesus. As a result, the entire city was enraged. People railed against Paul because he was teaching about Christ and the power of God. And yet *"many of those who had practiced magic brought their books together and burned them in the sight of all"* (Acts 19:19). And then, verse 20 tells us, *"So the word of the Lord grew mightily and prevailed."*

True revival is so disruptive that is confronts, destroys, and prevails over every other god. True revival is an open declaration that says, *"Jesus is King!"* We must also understand the revival that is coming is going to remove all the gray areas in the Church. It will provoke rage and chaos in the earth in the same way it did in Ephesus. The sin of man and the rage of satan will erupt when the Holy Spirit is poured out.

That sentence in Acts 19:20, *"The word of the Lord grew mightily and prevailed,"* is one of the clearest pictures of what happens in a season of revival. The revelation of the majesty of Jesus snowballs into a region, toppling down and prevailing over every other ideology and idolatry.

Billy: Now, again, I don't want to minimize the eternal truth of carrying the Holy Spirit within us and what that means as far as impacting lives and the world. The Holy Spirit's ministry inside us, in a way, impacts us on a smaller scale of what Corey is talking about that happens in entire cities. In fact, His presence in our lives awakens us to a realm of possibilities of glory and renewal we can walk in day in and day out and carry to others. I believe those who say, "I'm revival now," are touching on this very important truth of what is available to us now by the Holy Spirit's indwelling. But we can't leave it there. There's a greater scope to revival that we want to reach for, and that is a glory invasion across cities and regions. We desperately need His massive inbreaking right now! The Church should live pressing in for both realities.

Corey: I think it's really important to clear up some confusion regarding revival and another phrase, "open Heaven." I hear so many people using the phrase, and we need to understand there is a difference between an individual open Heaven and a corporate open Heaven. Revival is the season when the two become one.

This is what our mutual friend, Allen Hood, talks about so brilliantly when He discusses the concept of an open Heaven. There was an open Heaven at Jesus' baptism:

And suddenly a voice came from heaven, saying, "This is My beloved Son, in whom I am well pleased." (Matthew 3:17)

And there is an open Heaven on day one of salvation. As believers on day one, we're given access to the Third Person of the Trinity dwelling in us. We have received God's name as His children adopted into His family. We have the rights of His Kingdom. We can move in Kingdom authority and power. In other words, everything in the Kingdom is instantly available to us upon salvation. We're under an open Heaven, and we walk in it. We must not lose sight of being under an open Heaven, and we must awaken the Church to this reality once again—just to get back to normalcy. This should be our Christian *normal*.

It's one thing for me to have an open Heaven over me. It's another thing for my neighbors to have it over them. My unsaved neighbors, my unsaved city, my unsaved business, my unsaved school, and my unsaved region and country must come underneath the manifest presence of God. That's what we want to contend for.

We rest in the security of a believer. I rest in that. You rest in that. I don't have to contend for that for myself. I have it. You don't have to contend for it for yourself. You have it. We've been born again into it. We've been adopted as sons and daughters of God. But we contend for that regional open Heaven for all those around us.

Looking back at what happened after Jesus' baptism, Jesus was driven by the Holy Spirit into the wilderness, where He fasted for forty days and nights and overcame the adversary's every attempt to tempt Him (see Matthew 4). Luke 4 then tells us,

> *Then Jesus returned in the power of the Spirit to Galilee, and news of Him went out through all the surrounding region. And He taught in their synagogues, being glorified by all.* (vv. 14–15)

What happened according to these verses? There was an open Heaven over Galilee. Power and revival were hitting the region, and Jesus was *"being glorified by all"* after He fasted and contended with the devil for forty days and nights.

We need theological understanding of what we have—or who we have residing in us—and what we must do. We must raise the bar.

If we don't get this clear, we will continue to see any sort of prayer, fasting, and contending as religious striving because, "We've already got it." We do have it personally, but we don't corporately. That's what we contend for.

Billy: Absolutely! I want to dive deeper into the idea of us being God's children and the Father's affirmation of His Son before men. I believe the attack that Jesus faced by satan in the wilderness was an attack firstly upon Jesus' Sonship. This is something that the apostle Paul went after in his letter to the Galatians. He said,

> *Now I say that the heir, as long as he is a child, does not differ at all from a slave, though he is master of all, but is under guardians and stewards until the time appointed by the father. Even so we, when we*

were children, were in bondage under the elements of the world. But when the fullness of the time had come, God sent forth His Son, born of a woman, born under the law, to redeem those who were under the law, that we might receive the adoption as sons. And because you are sons, God has sent forth the Spirit of His Son into your hearts, crying out, "Abba, Father!" Therefore you are no longer a slave but a son, and if a son, then an heir of God through Christ. (Galatians 4:1–7)

God put the Spirit of His Son in our hearts—so that we can cry out, *"Abba, Father!"* The reality of the new birth is grander than any of us are even believing right now. However, the new birth inside us is not an awakening that covers a fifty-mile radius. It is powerful, but it is not an Isaiah 64 rent Heaven, where God rips everything open and comes down. Beloved, that's what we want you to see and understand theologically. The indwelling Spirit is just a down payment of the glory we will receive when the Lord is revealed. There is something God wants to release in this age where He manifests His Kingdom in power across regions, and we want to lift your vision higher—for you to have a vision of revival that lines up with what God has promised.

Paul said,

Now, therefore, you are no longer strangers and foreigners, but fellow citizens with the saints and members of the household of God, having been built on the foundation of the apostles and prophets,

Jesus Christ Himself being the chief cornerstone, in whom the whole building, being fitted together, grows into a holy temple in the Lord, in whom you also are being built together for a dwelling place of God in the Spirit. (Ephesians 2:19–22)

A tabernacle of glory—that's what we're being made into. First, we individually are a temple for the glory, but then we're being built into a corporate tabernacle to house His presence. What does this mean? It means we have access to the glory individually, we have access to it when we gather, and we have access to it regionally and globally. Get this biblical vision of revival where the planet is invaded by the glory.

So, we want to say *yes* to the incredible truth of the indwelling Spirit while saying *yes* simultaneously to a regional and global outpouring that transforms us and society and ushers in the return of the Lord. That's what Corey and I want you to get a vision for. We want you to get a vision of what the truth of the indwelling glory filling the city in which you live looks like. We want you to begin to see the very real possibility of that glory filling the businesses and schools in your region. What if the glory fell on your college campus? Can you imagine seeing a hundred, a thousand even, students and faculty slain under the glory?

We need to dream about what God can do. I pray that God lifts the bar of your understanding and lifts your vision higher than it's ever been before as to what His glory coming can look like. Let's get a high vision together of what His full invasion can be and allow that to become our vision for revival. That's what we want you to tap into.

5

WHAT REVIVAL LOOKS LIKE

Let's revisit the definition of revival that we introduced in the introduction:

> Revival is a divine season where God openly manifests the rule and reign of His Son by the outpouring of the Holy Spirit and the release of apostolic preaching. It's a snapshot of the coming day when the heavens are rent and God comes down, dismantling the powers of darkness and loosing satan's hold over the earth.

In revival, Jesus takes center stage and openly manifests His will and His Kingdom. And what we experience in revival isn't normal Christianity. The scope and the breadth of the impact are expansive. It's a massive explosion of glory from an open Heaven.

Corey: Think about God hitting your city with revival like He did Ephesus. There's apostolic preaching that's convicting everyone of sin. Picture it in your mind's eye. Your neighbors begin bringing all their "idols" to the city square in response to the Holy Spirit convicting them. They carry with them their pornography-laden literature, iPhones, iPads, and computers. They bring their drugs, bongs, and other paraphernalia, dumping them all at the downtown square.

Can you see the people of your city setting the stuff all on fire? Everything begins to crackle and pop as the fire rushes through the heap of trash.

Do you see your neighbors weeping and crying out to God for forgiveness?

Can you see drug dealers and pimps turning themselves into the cops because of the weight of conviction resting on them?

Do you understand what must happen in the human heart to get to that place of separating itself from what it lusts after and longs for?

Billy: Something that is so striking to me is how God will breathe on preaching and cause men's hearts to bend and then shatter underneath the weight of conviction. That's what we're talking about when we say, "apostolic preaching." It's preaching like the apostles released. It's preaching that has Heaven's weight upon it. It goes beyond a good message or a new revelation. Instead, it might be a topic that people have heard before, but in revival the glory of the Lord is resting on the spoken word. And instead of simply nudging or prodding the heart to change, the thunder of Heaven resounds in the message. They're the same human words, but they're carrying a weight of glory and striking the heart like a sledgehammer striking an anvil. It breaks people right where they sit, and wrecked by the hammer stroke, they run for forgiveness.

Corey: I've been in a few meetings where people threw their iPhones down at the front of a church's altar area. I watched them as they were struck by and grieved over their sin. Now, think about an entire city getting hit by that—by corporate repentance. Everything that each person has hidden has come to light. Everyone is owning their junk, burning it, and repenting completely of it. That's what happened in Ephesus, but you need to think about how that could look in our day.

Billy: Acts 19 tells us Paul preached boldly in the Ephesian synagogue for three months. He was pounding away at the Jews until some of their leaders became irritated with his messages. So, he took a group that had believed and began preaching and teaching them in a private lecture hall. He did this daily for the next two years. It was through these meetings that God cracked the stronghold over the city, and everyone in the region heard the gospel. They were also hearing the stories of the healings and miracles that were taking place through Paul.

The revival exploded when the sons of Sceva tried to use Jesus' name the way Paul did to drive out a demon. Instead of deliverance, they were beaten by the man with the demonic spirit. That moment caused the fear of God to fall on the *entire city*. Can you imagine an entire city coming under the tangible fear of the Lord? That's what we need to get a vision for! Our cities under the weight of His Glory. This is ultimately what caused them all to confess their sins and burn their idols.

Corey: People not only got rid of their idols, but they stopped buying new ones. Jesus was at the center of all their worship. So, the idol-making industry dried up in their city, and all the money that people and businesses made by their idol-making dried up as well.

When we see a principality broken like this, the principality loses its power but then begins to possess those who have resisted the gospel. They get mad and begin to incite violence. They look for someone they can harm. Maybe it's you or a neighbor whom they target. That's what happens when a principality gets cracked because of revival in your city. I want you to see that.

Billy: What is actually happening as people are incited against you or your neighbor is spiritual warfare. Though the crowd or mob doesn't realize it, the principality or power is directing their hostility to take it out on you. Paul wrote to the Ephesians, saying,

> *For we do not wrestle against flesh and blood, but against principalities, against powers, against the rulers of the darkness of this age, against spiritual hosts of wickedness in the heavenly places.* (Ephesians 6:12)

What was Paul saying? He was breaking down the degrees of demonic authority. There are principalities. There are powers. There are rulers of the darkness of this age. And there are spiritual hosts of wickedness in the heavens. The good news is Jesus is over and above them all because He has authority over them all. We read this in Colossians 2:10, where Paul said that Jesus *"is the head of all principality and power."* All authority and power have been given to Him.

Now, as a part of His Church, you must recognize Christ Jesus has given you weapons to use against the enemy and all his cohorts. You have the weapons of intercession, fasting, proclamation of the Word, and living out the value system of the Kingdom of God. When you walk out Kingdom values in your day-to-day life, it takes back the authority the enemy absconded. I want to remind you of something else about the weapons you have. The apostle Paul said you don't war according to the flesh because the weapons of your warfare...

> *Are not carnal but mighty in God for pulling down strongholds, casting down arguments and every high thing that exalts itself against the knowledge of God, bringing every thought into captivity to the obedience of Christ, and being ready to punish all disobedience when your obedience is fulfilled.*
> (2 Corinthians 10:4–6)

Every thought and vain argument that tries to usurp and exalt itself above Christ are brought under Christ as we cast them down.

So, when God moves in revival and the adversary begins to lash out at you, remember your weaponry. Pull down strongholds. Cast down arguments, and take captive every thought, bringing it to obedience to Christ.

> *Finally, my brethren, be strong in the Lord and in the power of His might. Put on the whole armor of God, that you may be able to stand against the wiles of the devil.* (Ephesians 6:10–11)

Corey: Beloved, what we saw in Acts 19 is going to happen all over the earth. That's why it's critical you begin to envision it. Acts 19 is going to go global!

Billy: Just mark this. Apostolic preaching is what cracks principalities. When Paul was talking about breaking strongholds, he was talking about doing it through proclaiming truth that casts down the lies. And when the strongholds crack, the enemy gets enraged. When you see massive persecution of Christians, it's because a principality is losing its grip. And we always see revival met with massive persecution. This must be part of your vision for revival.

Corey: From the very beginning of the book of Acts, we see the biblical preparation for seasons of revival; it's corporate prayer and fasting. In John 20, Jesus breathed on them and told them to receive the Holy Spirit. In Acts 1, He commanded them not to depart from Jerusalem but to wait for the Holy Spirit because they would be baptized in the Holy Spirit in a matter of days. The promise of the Father is the outpouring of the Holy Spirit. The dream of the Father is Him getting closer to us.

In Acts 2, we find the 120 waiting in the upper room as Jesus had instructed them before His ascension. They were there for ten days, praying and fasting. And they were united in purpose. We read:

> *And suddenly there came a sound from heaven, as of a rushing mighty wind, and it filled the whole house where they were sitting. Then there appeared to them divided tongues, as of fire, and one sat upon each of them. And they were all filled with the Holy Spirit and began to speak with other tongues, as the Spirit gave them utterance.* (Acts 2:2–4)

Please don't read past these verses. Christianity was birthed in a corporate prayer meeting.

They heard a sound of a rushing mighty wind.

The sound filled the house.

Divided tongues of fire sat on them.

They were filled with the Holy Spirit.

They spoke in tongues.

And Jesus would thrust these 120 unqualified people out of the upper room down to where all the Jews from every nation were milling about.

Peter, the one who fifty days earlier had denied Jesus, stood up and preached the first message, and three thousand were *"cut to the heart"* and basically cried out, "What must we do to be saved?" (see Acts 2:37).

is when God anoints the unqualified with a bold-
ᴖ a power that cuts. We desperately need preaching
ᴖat cuts. That's what happens in revival. The Word cuts.

God, we long for this season to come. Release words that cut. Release apostolic messengers and apostolic preaching once again!

6

REVIVAL AND THE
END OF THE AGE

Now that we have a clearer vision for what revival looks like, there's something a bit sobering that we need to understand. Here's the deal. If we want the real thing—true revival—it won't necessarily end with us increasing and becoming awesome. What will happen to us may look more like what happened to John the Baptist who said Jesus *"must increase, but I must decrease"* (John 3:30).

When the Spirit was poured out at Ephesus in Acts 19, verse 10 tells us that *"all who dwelt in Asia heard the word of the Lord Jesus, both Jews and Greeks."* As we have seen, Paul preached Christ. The Word of God prevailed. Miracles broke out. Healings via handkerchiefs happened. And all the witchcraft paraphernalia was brought into the city's center and burned. The idol-making industry and principality associated with it were overturned. Under this open Heaven, tumult filled the city. Those whose hearts remained hardened to the gospel suddenly wanted to stop the revival. They wanted to grab some people and kill them. In fact, they seized two of Paul's travel companions along with another Jew who just happened to be in the crowd (see Acts 19:29, 33). For two hours, the crowd shouted, *"Great is Diana of the Ephesians!"* (v. 34).

What was going on? The people were incited by the dethroned principality to try to stop the revival by taking the leaders out.

Martyrdom, that's what can happen when true revival breaks out upon a region. In all our excitement and anticipation of what we can expect revival to look like, it behooves us to remember persecution is sent to stem the tide of the outpouring, and it may even result in believers being martyred.

At the end of the age, along with the great harvest and global revival, the great tribulation will come. It will be global revival and great persecution, massive harvest and the martyrdom of the saints. But we also need to keep in mind that Jesus will return for His Bride, and all of hell being unleashed against her and Him will not stop Him. Remember, He wins!

Billy: My whole understanding of the end times used to be that revival will happen—a big, global revival. That's all I knew. I thought massive revival will come and then we all get to go be with Jesus. I had no understanding of the biblical narrative regarding the end of the age and the age to come.

After much study, I came to realize there is a shocking drama that will unfold as we wrap up this age. It will include outpouring and judgment. Glory and tribulation. God's mighty blessing and satan's illogical rage. Here is what we must understand: There is an end-time ingathering of souls that will take place across every tribe, tongue, people, and nation in conjunction with massive shakings, trials, and tribulation.

When we look at Revelation 7, there is this very interesting conversation between John and one of the elders near the throne:

> *Then one of the elders answered, saying to me, "Who are these arrayed in white robes, and where did they come from?" And I said to him, "Sir, you know." So he said to me, "These are the ones who come out of the great tribulation, and washed their robes and made them white in the blood of the Lamb. Therefore they are before the throne of God, and serve Him day and night in His temple. And He who sits on the throne will dwell among them."* (vv. 13–15)

This shows us that there is an end-time ingathering that will hit the planet. It will touch every single people group— every tribe, tongue, people, and nation. And it will happen *during* the great tribulation, the last three-and-a-half years of this age. It was what Peter was talking about in Acts 2:

*But this is what was spoken by the prophet Joel: "And
it shall come to pass in the last days, says God, that
I will pour out of My Spirit on all flesh; your sons
and your daughters shall prophesy, your young men
shall see visions, your old men shall dream dreams.
And on My menservants and on My maidser-
vants I will pour out My Spirit in those days; and
they shall prophesy. I will show wonders in heaven
above and signs in the earth beneath: blood and
fire and vapor of smoke. The sun shall be turned
into darkness, and the moon into blood, before the
coming of the great and awesome day of the Lord.
And it shall come to pass that whoever calls on the
name of the Lord shall be saved." (vv. 16–21)*

Corey: Peter was saying that Joel's prophecy had begun and
would continue until the great and awesome day of the Lord.
What we see laid out in Acts 2 is the biblical model for seeing
seasons of revival break in, leading us to the return of the
Lord. Gatherings of prayer, fasting and repentance—all lead
to fresh outpourings of the Holy Spirit, which in turn lead to
the return of Jesus.

This is why Acts 3:19, which we referenced earlier, is so
important because we can't divorce revival from the return of
the Lord as they are inextricably connected.

*Repent therefore and be converted, that your sins
may be blotted out, so that times of refreshing may
come from the presence of the Lord, and that* [the
Father] *may send Jesus Christ, who was preached*

> *to you before, whom heaven must receive until the times of restoration of all things, which God has spoken by the mouth of all His holy prophets since the world began.* (Acts 3:19–21)

My ultimate longing for revival is for Jesus to come back, and I know from Scripture that revival expedites His return.

Billy: So, there is a global awakening that is going to happen in conjunction with all the drama of the end times. According to the Scripture, we will see massive outpourings and judgments. They will happen together as God is able to do multiple things at once. He is able to bring in a great harvest while many are falling away. He is able to pour out His Spirit in fire and glory across the nations while judging the sin of humanity. And He will do all these things in concert with one another.

It is very important that you understand what is happening and what is coming because this will help you calibrate how you live right now. Does how you live today make sense in light of the future outpouring that is going to cover the globe, the future global judgment, the future rage of satan, and the future massive harvest? The drama is getting ready to unfold in the earth, and how you live your life right now needs to make sense in light of all these things.

Corey: You see, most of us think that all our problems disappear when revival comes. But true biblical revival actually picks a fight. It confronts us. It confronts the principalities and rulers of darkness of this age. It removes the gray areas. It's like what Jesus said,

And this is the condemnation, that the light has come into the world, and men loved darkness rather than light, because their deeds were evil. For everyone practicing evil hates the light and does not come to the light, lest his deeds should be exposed. (John 3:19–20)

The Light, the Second Person of the Trinity, stepped down onto the planet. Talk about revival! The Light had come into the world, and humanity—in the light of that full-blinding, blazing Light—wanted darkness because we were afraid our evil deeds would be exposed. Humanity likes to live perpetually in the gray and dark areas—in the in-between spaces. But revival shines the Light and draws some people to it while it repels others.

As the earth prepares for this same Light to step back onto planet, we are going to see increasing measures of Light invade the earth that will result in extreme love for God and extreme hatred for God.

There will be two harvests at the end of the age.

Jesus told us about the great harvest that will come at the end of the age: the harvest of the wheat *and* the tares. This will provoke those who prefer darkness like it did in Acts 19, like it did in Jesus' ministry, and like it did in historic revivals and great awakenings. We love the revival glory stories, but most of us don't talk about, for example, how most of Wales hated Evan Roberts, the Welsh revivalist, or how great resistance came against the Azusa Street revival and, before it, the Second Great Awakening in upstate New York.

Revival outpouring, the gross sin of humanity, and the rage of satan happen simultaneously. In the last days, as satan loses his authority, he will have to release an all-out ground assault. He will manifest through men and women who will have given themselves over to darkness—who love darkness. The devil will operate through them. We will see persecution—the rage of satan—come against God's people. But we will also see the righteous judgments of God as He openly manifests His zeal and justice against evil and wickedness.

What kickstarts all of this? Revival!

I believe God is currently reawakening the Church to His vision for revival. He is restructuring the Church into a new wineskin, moving us into a new way and form that's not church as usual, as we've said. Acts 2 is going to be released on the earth. There is going to be stadium Christianity with masses of people gathering. There is going to be the manifestation of the glory of the Lord *"as the waters cover the sea"* (Hab. 2:14).

Billy: When you turn the light on, darkness flees. And as we embrace Light, we become light, and our light that we shine begins to expose *"the unfruitful works of darkness."* Paul spoke about this when he said:

> *For you were once darkness, but now you are the light in the Lord. Walk as children of light.... And have no fellowship with the unfruitful works of darkness, but rather expose them. For it is shameful even to speak of those things which are done by them in secret. But all things that are exposed are made*

manifest by the light, for whatever makes manifest is light. (Ephesians 5:8–13)

Paul went on to say, *"Awake, you who sleep, arise from the dead, and Christ will give you light"* (v. 14). Paul was giving a vision of what it looks like when the light and glory of the Lord are released. When light is released, it exposes darkness. These are two realities that happen in tandem.

I must confess that, when I was younger, the vision I had of revival had me as a superstar. But here's what God did with me. He gave me some "appetizers" of revival in my ministry. The power would come on me and come through me like I had never experienced. Then God would turn it off for six or nine months. He would allow me to sense my utter feebleness without His glory. I learned through this process that, when God releases an outpouring, it is not a testimony about the messenger. It is not a testimony about our personal "awesomeness." It is only and always to testify of His Son's name and glory.

When God releases an outpouring, He does it through flesh, through jars of clay. The treasure is released through *"earthen vessels,"* as Paul said, *"that the excellence of the power may be of God and not of us"* (2 Cor. 4:7). And that's the point: The glory is of Him, and it's not of us. He has had to turn it on and turn it off in my life many times so that I could finally come to the place where He increases and I don't. In fact, I decrease. He was using the outpouring of His Spirit through me to expose the unfruitfulness of pride inside me. In true revival, He is the only One who gets the glory.

John 3:30

The Lord alone will be exalted in the harvest at the end of the age. He will be exalted in His return. He alone is exalted in any true revival. And so, as you're getting a vision of revival, beloved, let me caution you from my experience. I became the star of my own vision. But there is only one Star in the Kingdom of God. There is only one exalted Name in the Kingdom of God. That Person is Jesus Christ. It's not the name of a church or a denomination or a preacher. All the thrones of the earth are infinitely beneath the Throne that is established in Heaven. And there is only one Name that the Father is zealous about the unanimous exaltation of—Jesus Christ.

The mass glorification of Jesus Christ is ultimately what the spirit of revival is all about.

We have to realize there is a great and terrible day of the Lord coming. The earth and Heaven will be shaken (see Luke 21:26; Heb. 12:26). Everything that can be shaken in that day will be shaken, and only those things that withstand God's shaking will remain. His only Son will be exalted for all to see on that day. When His judgments come to the earth, people learn righteousness. When the glory of the Lord is seen, all flesh is diminished in His presence. That's where all of this is going. The Father is zealous for the ultimate and full release of His Son's glory in the earth. This is the spirit of revival.

7

OUR PART IN THE END-TIME DRAMA

Too often, the role of revival in the end times has been misunderstood. Many have known there will be an end-time harvest or ingathering that will be the byproduct of a great outpouring of God's Spirit. However, the Church has not always done well in getting the big picture of how the end-time drama includes the greatest revival that will ever hit the earth.

We must see that the outpouring we are contending for is unto the return of the Lord. As we have established, global revival is a part of the end-time drama. We must get the picture of this unfolding drama not only to enhance our overall vision of revival in the context of the end times, but also to see the part we play in the drama itself.

Revival and the drama of the end of the age are deeply connected to the Church's intercession. Without the Bride partnering with Jesus in focused and prevailing prayer, there will be no end-time outpouring. Understanding our part in revival and in the end times will provoke us to prepare and pray now. It will stir the groan of intercession and enflame a passion for the knowledge of God. It will enable us to engage with the Lord to dethrone principalities and powers with the help of angelic hosts as we contend for the final breakthrough that will sweep, perhaps, a billion souls into the Kingdom of God.

Billy: Corey and I have had a similar journey. God marked us for revival, and then over time He began to color in the picture of what the revival He has planned entails. It took me a long time to realize that there is a "big R" revival that is unto Jesus' return. There will be many outpourings and seasons of refreshing, but there is a day coming that will see souls saved from every tribe, tongue, people, and nation. This mighty day of visitation is a day in our future and is so established in Scripture that we literally don't need any more prophetic words to tell us it is coming. We just need to believe the Bible.

Revelation 12 is a wild chapter that encapsulates what is coming in a dramatic way. A woman is introduced in Revelation 12, and she is giving birth to a male child. A dragon with seven heads and ten horns appears in this chapter, and we see he's coming to devour the child. The passage culminates with the male child being scooped up to Heaven, and the dragon, which is lucifer, is enraged. So, the dragon goes to make war against the offspring of the woman, who are the believers in Jesus and the Jewish nation.

Revelation 12 gives us this metaphorical scene that speaks powerfully to what will happen in the last three-and-one-half years of this age. And we are shown this scene for a purpose. We need to know the biblical narrative of what is coming at the end of the age to instruct our hearts and breathe into us vision for revival and the Lord's return. If we do not see the role of revival in the end times, we won't have the big picture of what we need to contend for.

When you begin to get your mind around that vision in Revelation 12, you realize it's speaking of a time that will be the most dynamic and dramatic time in human history. A war will break out in Heaven, Michael and his angels will fight the dragon (satan), and the dragon and his angels will not win. We read:

> *And war broke out in heaven: Michael and his angels fought with the dragon; and the dragon and his angels fought, but they did not prevail, nor was a place found for them in heaven any longer. So the great dragon was cast out, that serpent of old, called the devil and satan, who deceives the whole world; he was cast to the earth, and his angels were cast out with him. Then I heard a loud voice saying in heaven, "Now salvation, and strength, and the kingdom of our God, and the power of His Christ have come, for the accuser of our brethren, who accused them before our God day and night, has been cast down."* (Revelation 12:7–10)

eady, the devil has been cast into the third Heaven, the
⸱ of God, in Zion, the Heavenly City. He was cast from
ᴜ⸱ ⸱e into the second heaven. This is where he is right now. But
there is a day coming when satan will be cast out of the second
heaven to the earth, *"having great wrath, because he knows that
he has a short time"* (Rev. 12:12).

Corey: I want to connect Revelation 12 with Daniel 10. In
Daniel 10, we see Daniel as an old man in a season of prayer
and fasting for twenty-one days. He was going after God,
seeking God's purposes for the future of Israel, and desiring
Israel to be fully established in her land.

> *In those days I, Daniel, was mourning three full
> weeks. I ate no pleasant food, no meat or wine came
> into my mouth, nor did I anoint myself at all, till
> three whole weeks were fulfilled.* (Daniel 10:2–3)

On the twenty-first day, a mighty angel appeared and said
to Daniel,

> *Do not fear, Daniel, for from the first day that you
> set your heart to understand, and to humble your-
> self before your God, your words were heard; and I
> have come because of your words.* (Daniel 10:12)

Then the angel said something extraordinary:

> *But the prince of the kingdom of Persia withstood
> me twenty-one days; and behold, Michael, one of
> the chief princes, came to help me, for I had been*

> *left alone there with the kings of Persia.* (Daniel 10:13)

At the very beginning when Daniel set about to seek God, the angel was sent to bring a message to him but was prevented by an angelic war with the principality or prince over Persia. For twenty-one days, the angel was fighting against this principality. Meanwhile, Daniel kept showing up, day after day, praying and fasting, confessing the Word, and repenting for his people in intercession. But the angel couldn't break through to deliver the message to Daniel, so God sent Michael, the chief prince over Israel, to enter into a war in the second heaven. When Michael showed up, the angel broke through and appeared before Daniel.

This is an amazing picture!

Billy: It shows us what happens when we are faithful with fasting and prayer. We may not physically see anything happening in our favor. We may not feel anything. But Daniel 10 lets us know, as we fast and pray, angels and demons, principalities and powers are shifting and moving. I love reading verse 12 where Daniel is told the angel came because of Daniel's words! This tells us our words have the authority and power to move God and to move angels and demons in the unseen realm.

Think about that for a minute. What would have happened if Daniel had stopped on day eight or day ten? What would have happened if he fasted until day twenty and then stopped? Daniel 10 demonstrates what happens when we stay in the place of fasting and prayer, when we remain faithful in intercession to the end—it brings breakthrough.

From Daniel 10 through 12, we are given one of the most prolific, end-time revelations imaginable. The angel unpacked centuries' worth of revelation of what will happen on the earth. But here's what I want you to see. We are given the pictorial of what happens in the heavens when people of God cry out with fasting and prayer. Now, let's take this information forward to Revelation 12, where the war broke out in the heavens. What does that tell us?

Corey: It shows us that there is a Daniel company on the earth who are in prayer and fasting and are maturing in their identity and understanding of what happens when their words, their prayers, their repentance, and their seeking God penetrate the unseen realm. What we are going to see is that there's not just going to be Daniel in Babylon or Persia, but there is going to be a global company—the whole Body of Christ—engaged in this place of prayer and fasting for the open Heaven.

What will this global Daniel company's intercession and travail produce? There won't be just one angel coming down because of their words. No, what happens is satan himself will be thrown out of the second heaven with all his demons. He will be cast down to the earth, and Heaven will be opened wide. A global open Heaven will ensue. This is what will characterize the last three-and-one-half years of this age.

Billy: This vision has been a consuming vision for me. It's the reason we do 24/7 live worship and prevailing prayer at

GateCity in Atlanta. We are interceding for that day of massive breakthrough in the heavens across all the earth. This global open Heaven coincides with Joel's prophecy about God's Spirit being poured out upon all humanity.

We need to see this for what it is. When satan is cast down, there is no demonic traffic in the second heaven, and without that disruptive traffic, we end up with a generation on the earth that not only has sourced the angelic realm through their intercession, but now gets to engage in the answer to their prayers. This means, at the end of the age, the Body of Christ will be operating in signs, wonders, and miracles in a measure that the earth has never seen.

Meanwhile, the adversary will be launching his ground war! He will have great rage because he knows his time is short. His only option will be to try to end the tide of revival by martyring those responsible.

As Revelation 11 informs us, there will be two witnesses who testify and prophesy with great power. In fact, Revelation 11:6 says they will have power over weather, power to turn water into blood, and power *"to strike the earth with all plagues, as often as they desire."* They will move in signs, wonders, and miracles as often as they wish. These two witnesses will lead a global company to bring the gospel to the nations of the earth. Jesus said the end would come when the gospel is *"preached in all the world as a witness to the nations"* (Matt. 24:14).

The global proclamation of the gospel, the global outpouring of the Holy Spirit, and the global open Heaven will all occur concurrently with satan being cast down and enraged as well as with the end-time judgments. Beloved, it will be the Church's finest hour. So, the way we're living right now—we must stress this again—must make sense in light of that future day or else our lives are disconnected from the unfolding plan of the Kingdom of God. I want to call you into that. I want you to recognize that you must engage now in a life of fasting and prayer, believing for breakthrough and the ultimate outpouring of the Spirit at the end of the age.

Corey: It's a matter of war. And you have been made for war. We have been made for war. But the enemy has domesticated this generation. He has anesthetized and medicated it. Where we should be learning how to fight the good fight of faith, how to see the Word of the Lord prevail, all in preparation for the greatest battle in history, we're sidelined. We need a Daniel company to arise with vision—a company who understands their spiritual weapons for breakthrough.

I want to connect all of this to Acts 19 and Ephesus. The gospel broke through in Ephesus. The principality was unseated and cast down. Persecution arose because the adversary raged. But a great ingathering followed. Now, look once again at Revelation 12 with me. It's the end picture for what the Church historically has done in her war with satan and in her participation in the spreading of the gospel. Verse 11 says, *"And they overcame him by the blood of the Lamb and by the word of their testimony, and they did not love their lives to the death."*

The global persecution that will result in satan being cast down to earth will be in the context of revival, stadium Christianity, two witnesses, power of God, and judgments of God. The devil will invest his resources into a man called the antichrist. The antichrist will become the devil's primary agent for the last three-and-one-half years of this age. And we will see the Church arise in the earth. We will see her participate in the incredible end-time drama.

Billy: It's the most beautiful story, and you have to let it grip you heart and soul. Our Jesus, our Bridegroom, dethroned lucifer at the cross by the power of His blood. He cast satan and his demonic hosts to the second heaven. *"Having disarmed principalities and powers, He made a public spectacle of them, triumphing over them in it"* (Col. 2:15). Access to the Father was given to us through His Son, Jesus Christ. The power of sin and death no longer has authority over those who are born again because of the work of the cross. So, Jesus triumphed over satan at the cross.

Now, watch this. Jesus has invited us, His Bride, into partnership with Him for the culmination of this age. The *they* who overcome satan in Revelation 12:11 is the Bride. That Jesus would dignify you and me in this way is mind-blowing. We get to stand with Him in intimacy and authority to deal the final death blow on satan in this age! *Oh, Jesus, it's marvelous!*

And how will we overcome the adversary? By the blood of Jesus, by the word of our testimony, *and* not loving our lives unto death. His blood cleanses us and gives us power to stand in and for righteousness. Then our testimony—not wavering in boldness, not wavering in our stand for righteousness—declares who He is and what He's done. And finally, just as Jesus laid down His life for His Bride, we get to lay down our lives for Him.

Listen, friend, we are afraid of many silly things. I want you to know there is a love that is stronger than death. There is a jealousy that is crueler than the grave. There is a power in the love of Jesus to liberate your soul from fear. The only way the Church at the end of the age is going to lay down her life is through her loving Jesus more than herself. It's going to be the love we have for Jesus that enables us to withstand suffering and even death. It's going to be our finest hour. It's going to be the greatest time of Kingdom manifestation. And the beauty of the whole story is that Jesus would invite us into it with Him. He doesn't finalize satan's defeat apart from us. He does it through us. This is the wonder of what it means to be joined with Him in His story. Ultimately, this is our role in the end-time drama.

8

GOD'S DREAM

As the Bridegroom's partner in the end-time drama, we want to be in close and intimate communion with Him. We want always to be with Him, to walk with Him, and to know Him. We want our hearts gripped with love for Him.

In this partnership, we want to be so intoxicated with our love for Jesus that we no longer see revival through some self-serving lens. Instead, we want to see revival with lovesick eyes, longing for Jesus to be known in His beauty and desiring that He receive the full reward of His suffering. Revival is the outcome of a bridal partnership wherein we love Him completely and carry His burdens.

When we love Him this deeply, it causes us to want to know what He wants. We want to understand what it is that

He is longing for. When we love Him for Him instead of for us and what we can get from Him, we can then begin to seek Him in the intimacy of asking, "Lord, what is Your dream? What is it You're longing for?" When we get those answers, when He vulnerably invites us into His desires, we are getting to the heart of God for revival. It's then that we can allow Him to wreck our lives for nothing less than the complete fulfillment of His dream, of His heart's desire. It's about connecting with the longings in Jesus' heart and letting His longings become our own. This is what we see in David.

Corey: I believe the greatest longing in God is to fully dwell on the earth with His people. This is what we see in the garden, and it's what we will see at the descent of the New Jerusalem as God "tabernacles" among us. Very few in history have connected to this longing, and even fewer have thrown their lives into the intercession to see the fullness of it manifested in their generation. David is one of the few who did it, and his intercession changed history.

King David was a man after God's own heart (see 1 Sam. 13:14; Acts 13:22). At thirty-seven years of age, he became king in Jerusalem and stepped into the fullness of his promise. In Second Samuel 7:1, we are told that the Lord had given David rest from all his enemies. What separated David from everyone else in his generation is, after he had entered into the fullness of his promise and was resting, he noticed that God wasn't resting, and that bothered him. He said to Nathan the prophet, *"See now, I dwell in a house of cedar, but the ark of God dwells inside tent curtains"* (2 Sam. 7:2).

That night, God spoke to Nathan about what David had said. He told Nathan to ask David,

> *Would you build a house for Me to dwell in? For I have not dwelt in a house since the time that I brought the children of Israel up from Egypt, even to this day, but have moved about in a tent and in a tabernacle . . . have I ever spoken a word to anyone from the tribes of Israel, whom I commanded to shepherd My people Israel, saying, "Why have you not built Me a house of cedar?"* (2 Samuel 7:5–7)

I remember years ago when I was reading this verse, and it hit me very strongly that God wasn't saying, "Would you?" but He was actually saying, "You mean, you would?"

David wanted to give God something that God had never articulated or made known, but because David was a man after God's heart, he knew what God wanted and wanted to give it to Him.

This is what separates David from everybody else. He had come into "his promises," but he wasn't satisfied until God got His. I believe David touched the ancient, eternal longing in the heart of God to fully dwell on the earth with His sons and daughters. When David expressed that, a volcano erupted in God's heart toward David, which resulted in God telling Nathan to let David know He was going to build David a house. It would be a house and kingdom established forever. When David touched the heart of God, God made an everlasting covenant with David.

David wanted to build God a house. God flipped the table and declared to David that He was going to build him a house that would endure forever and that the Messiah would sit on his throne.

This is central to our theme of revival because revival isn't just a manifestation of Jesus the Son of God in Heaven, but it is a declaration that He is coming to rule on the earth as the Son of David.

Billy: What we are touching on is one of the deepest longings in the heart of God. If you dug deeply into God's heart, you would find just how much He desires to be with us, His people. We see it in the garden in Genesis. We see it in Moses' tabernacle. And then David shifts everything in his tabernacle of worship. We see it again in Solomon's temple. And we see it more fully expressed in the God-Man, Jesus. God came and tabernacled with us. He dwelt among us.

The truth told throughout the Scripture is this—God wants to dwell with us. He gives us the Holy Spirit, not to just be near us or on us. He gives the Holy Spirit to live inside us. Something is continually moving in the heart of the Father that is so tender and deep that He wants to be with us—this is His dream. And the ultimate expression or fulfillment of God's dream will occur after the Lord Jesus returns to rule and reign in Jerusalem and the Father ultimately makes His dwelling place among us once again. He's bringing everything back to what He had with Adam in the garden (see Rev. 21:1–4).

When we look at the heart of David, we begin to recognize that David touched this deep place in the heart of God. He connected with God's desire to be with us. This desire is something central to all worship and worship environments. We sing to Him and love Him, not because we first loved Him, but because He first loved us and longs to be with us. He authors the longing within us to love and adore Him and then meets us in that place, because He wants to be with us. Psalm 132 portrays how David lived his entire life under a vow to fulfill God's dream of dwelling with us.

In Psalm 80, Asaph said, and I'm paraphrasing, "You who live among the cherubim, don't stay up there. Come here and shine forth among your people. Tabernacle and dwell with us." So, when we're talking about our having a vision for revival and seeing God's dream become a reality, we're talking about the dwelling place of God being among humanity. We're talking about what it looks like when God comes and resides in holy habitation among His people. Oh, I want to live connected to His desire to be with us and dwell among us.

Corey: Psalm 132 lays out David's vow that consumed his life, and this vow changed history. I believe the same vow will overcome the Church in the last days. In our day, such a vow declares war on the American dream so that the Heavenly dream can be realized in our generation.

> *Lord, remember David and all his afflictions; how he swore to the Lord, and vowed to the Mighty One of Jacob: "Surely I will not go into the chamber of my house, or go up to the comfort of my bed; I will not give sleep to my eyes or slumber to my eyelids, until I find a place for the Lord, a dwelling place for the Mighty One of Jacob." (Psalm 132:1–5)*

David would not rest until God rested. Solomon, who wrote this Psalm, watched his dad's life be consumed by this one desire: for God to have a dwelling place on the earth.

David wasn't acting out of some human zeal. He was not stirring something up in his own strength. He became possessed with God's zeal. He was possessed with what God has always wanted. He expressed this powerfully in Psalm 69:9, *"Because zeal for Your house has eaten me up, and the reproaches of those who reproach You have fallen on me."*

When zeal for God's resting place begins to eat you like a virus—when it gets all up inside you—it messes with your sleep. It messes with your eating. It messes with your dreams and goals. It consumes you.

In John 2, when Jesus cleansed the temple, all of the sudden the Holy Spirit hit those disciples, and they remembered Psalm 69. They realized Jesus looked a lot like His great-grandfather, David.

Beloved, David's vow is being released across the earth. The Psalm 132 vow, the longing for God to have a place, is being released into God's people today. Zeal for God's house pushes everything else out of the way in our hearts. It's no longer about my destiny or your destiny, or my calling or your calling. What happens is we begin to steward the ancient longing in God until it is realized. As we come closer to the Lord's return, that zeal is going to intensify.

Billy: David wasn't perfect. He probably had just crested into manhood when God said David was a man after His heart. He was this young thirteen-year-old, not much more than a boy in our eyes, singing love songs to God on the backside of

the desert while tending a few sheep. He was forgotten by his
father and despised by his brothers. But David had caught the
attention of Heaven. What was going on with him? He had
Heaven's attention even when his own family rejected him.
Whatever David tapped into moved the heart of God in a
way that is nearly unmatched in all of Scripture. David's longing compelled God to move. This is the same longing that
everyone who is hungry for revival carries. This ache is the
ache that moves Heaven.

What is it? It's this—David wanted the presence of God
more than he wanted anything else. He desired God more
than he wanted man's approval or any earthly platform. He
didn't want human praise. He wanted God's presence. King
Saul's problem was that he wanted man's approval. King David
wanted God's affirmation. King Saul was apprehended by his
own dreams. King David was apprehended by God's dream.

Beloved, get a vision for God's dream. Desire to give God
what He has desired. Be like David and let the zeal for God's
house consume you. It's this vision and dream, this longing
and desire, that sees revival birthed in a generation. When
David's vow finally came to fruition, it was at the dedication
of Solomon's temple. The vow that David made culminated
in physical fire falling from Heaven and an entire generation
bowing before God's glory. Oh, to see this in our day—
that we would get a vision for His habitation and see it in
our generation.

9

HISTORIC
TWENTIETH-CENTURY
REVIVALS

Perhaps the most impacting influences on our vision for revival are testimonies to how God has moved throughout history. More specifically, the written testimonies of men and women who have experienced great revivals of the past have helped us dare to dream about what God can and will do in the future.

We think the beloved apostle John was on to something when he ended his Gospel with these words:

And truly Jesus did many other signs in the presence of His disciples, which are not written in this book; but these are written that you may believe that Jesus is the Christ, the Son of God, and that believing you may have life in His name. (John 20:30–31)

John was touching on how a written record or testimony of Jesus' life and ministry can impact a reader's life. And that's why we have pointed you to the biblical record of revival. *"So then faith comes by hearing, and hearing by the word of God"* (Rom. 10:17). Though inspired by the Holy Spirit, John wrote motivated by the desire to cause others to believe. And that's the power of the testimony of God. It produces faith!

John later recorded, *"For the testimony of Jesus is the spirit of prophecy"* (Rev. 19:10). What is written in the biblical record—testifying to Jesus, His life, His words, and His acts—prophesy to what He is doing now and will do in the future. And that not only inspires hope and faith, but it also begins to create a picture of God-possibilities for us.

With that in mind, we want to share with you a few of our favorite testimonies of when God has moved powerfully in past revivals. We trust these stories will help lift your vision of what God can do and of what revival can look like. May the testimonies we share generate a seed of faith to believe for something more than you have ever seen or experienced.

Billy: Probably my favorite revival that I've ever read about—and I've read about thirty books on revival—is the Welsh revival. Led by Evan Roberts, this revival went from 1904 to about 1906. At the beginning, Roberts was twenty-six years old. And when I first read his story, I was the same age, and it did something in my heart, showing me at the time how God could use someone my age to impact a nation for Him. The story of the Welsh revival so profoundly touched me that four years later we named our first son, Evan, after Evan Roberts.

But let's look at the story. Evan Roberts felt a call into the ministry. So, he went to Bible school. Feeling the burden of God for his nation, he would have these moments where he was deeply gripped with travail and intercession. For example, during their Bible classes, there were times when he fell out of his chair in intercession while weeping and wailing in the classroom. His experience was so intense that the instructors didn't know what to do with him. They physically had him checked out by a medical doctor, who diagnosed Roberts with *religious mania*.[1] Finally, the instructors and leaders of the school decided to send Roberts home because he wasn't able to complete his studies and what he was doing in intercession and travail was disruptive.

Roberts went home and talked to his pastor about allowing him to preach to the church, but the pastor wasn't about to let him do that, especially after Roberts had been sent home by the Bible school. Roberts did manage to talk his pastor into letting him gather some young people together to pray. So, Roberts got about seventeen young people, ranging in age from about fifteen to twenty-something, to meet for prayer. Roberts and these young people began crying out for revival, and something soon broke open and began to spread. In a matter of weeks, other churches began to hear that something had happened with these young people who were meeting there in Loughor, Wales.

As a result, these churches invited Roberts and the youth to come and minister at their churches. And every single time, when Roberts and the youth conducted a service, they would just wait on the Holy Spirit. They would seek God. They would worship. And at some point, the conviction of the Lord would come through their singing and their intercession. And then Evan Roberts, he prayed this prayer: "Bend us, bend us, oh Lord." What he was saying was, "Bend us to Your will. Everything that doesn't conform to Your will, bend us." And he had this four-point sermon, in which he preached:

1. Confess and repent of all sin.
2. Remove any questionable thing in your life.
3. Promptly obey the Holy Spirit, doing whatever He tells you to do.
4. Publicly confess Christ as Savior.

Many times, people would pack into the meetings that Roberts led, and there would be as many people outside the meetings as there were inside. And again, Roberts would simply wait. He'd just sit there and wait on the Holy Spirit. And what was interesting, though a young man, he was not given to the pressure typically experienced by young men to perform. No, Roberts just waited on the Lord. This is a theme we see, not only in the Welsh revival with Roberts, but in other revivals like Azusa Street.

And so, the Welsh revival explodes. And one of my favorite testimonies about the revival came from the editor of this historic newspaper out of Great Britain, *The Pall Mall Gazette.* The editor of *The Pall Mall Gazette* went to Wales to do a story on the revival as it had started to get international notoriety. As he got off the train in Loughor, he asked directions to the revival. A young man told him to go down to the end of the street, turn left, and walk. The young man said the editor would begin to feel it. What the young man was alluding to was the haunting fear of the Lord that filled the city. The heat from the fire of God was felt in Loughor, Wales.

The editor was interviewed for the *Methodist Times* and was asked if he had been to the revival and what he thought of it. And this was the editor's response:

> The question is not what I think of it, but what it thinks of me, of yon, and all the rest of us. For it is a very real thing, this Revival: a live thing which seems to have a power and a grip which may get hold of a good many of us who at present are mere spectators.[2]

The Welsh revival shocked an entire nation. "It swept over the whole of Wales in an astonishingly short time, a movement of resistless, potent, cyclonic Divine power. By the end of 1905, it had spread, practically over the whole of the religious world."[3] And that revival is what Frank Bartleman envisioned in Los Angeles, leading into Azusa Street.

Corey: During the Welsh revival, Frank Bartleman was in Pasadena, California, and he and Roberts were writing to each other. And it's almost like the revival went from Wales to Azusa—like there was a transference. I love Frank Bartleman's account of the intercession that led up to Azusa Street.

In April of 1905, after Bartleman's daughter, Esther, had passed away in January, Bartleman heard F.B. Meyer preach, describing the revival happening in Wales. Bartleman wrote:

> My soul was stirred to its depths, having read of this revival shortly before. I then and there promised God He should have full right of way with me, if He could use me.
>
> I distributed tracts in the post office, banks, and public buildings in Los Angeles and also took tracts to many saloons. Later I visited about thirty saloons in Los Angeles again....
>
> Little Esther's death had broken my heart, and I felt I could live only while in God's service. I longed to know Him in a more real way and to see the work of God go forth in power. A great burden and cry came in my heart for a mighty revival.[4]

Bartleman fully resigned himself to see revival come to Los Angeles and Southern California. And it was really there, even after the death of his daughter, that he went all the way in to see God move in Pasadena and Los Angeles.

Bartleman began to write tracts and would hand them out to people. He was barely surviving as he and his family were living by faith. But what you see with Frank Bartleman was this growing spirit of intercession. It was the increase of what he would call *soul travail*.

Travail is a real hallmark of revival praying. It reminds us of the birthing process of natural children. When God is birthing a move of His Spirit, He moves upon His children in travail.

Bartleman's book, *Azusa Street*, has lines in it that are powerful and have deeply impacted me. He wrote:

> At night I could scarcely sleep for the spirit of prayer. I fasted much, not caring for food while burdened. At one time I was in soul travail for nearly twenty-four hours without intermission. It nearly used me up. Prayer literally consumed me. Sometimes I would groan all night in my sleep.[5]

And in his book, he recounted what he was reading and hearing about revivals not only in Wales, but in India as well. One line he shared about the revival in India changed my life. The line Bartleman penned found its source in *The Great Mukti Revival*, which reported on the revival at Pandita Ramabai's Mukti Mission, where girls and young women had experienced an incredible outpouring of the Holy Spirit. These ladies entered into "such intense seeking" that "could not have been endured save that it had been done in the power of the Spirit. They neither ate nor slept until the victory was won."[6] As Bartleman related the story, he said, "They forgot to eat and sleep."[7] That was the line that blew me away! I wondered what made Bartleman not care for food and these young women forget to eat and sleep, *What was that? When was the last time I forgot to sleep? When was the last time I forgot to eat?* And I was reading this, and I thought, *This dude and these ladies are possessed by the Spirit of God in a way that I don't know anything about.*

Bartleman carried this burden, and he met another who did as well. The man's name was Edward Boehmer, whom Bartleman called "Brother Boehmer." Bartleman had met Brother Boehmer at the Peniel Mission in Pasadena. Bartleman and Brother Boehmer had many all-night prayer meetings. At times, Boehmer would accompany Bartleman in handing out tracts; in fact, Brother Boehmer would stand outside saloons and intercede for Bartleman who went into the saloons to distribute tracts.

So, these two men were praying and sharing, and they were having visitations with Jesus. He was showing up to them. And there was this growing sense that the train was coming. The train was coming. And that is what we see building up with Bartleman's intercession. And then, right in the middle of that—Azusa Street began on April 9, 1906—but right in that season, the great earthquake shook San Francisco and was felt all the way down to Los Angeles.

What we see with all of these revivals is the significant timing of things. When God begins to come, we see a synergism of the groan of creation with the ripening of the sin of man and the harvest of souls in these seasons.

So, the earthquake in San Francisco happened, and Frank Bartleman wrote a tract through the night that he referred to as his "Earthquake" tract. And he began to go and share it with others, warning of the shaking and judgments of God. Preachers of the day were working overtime to say Azusa wasn't of God, but Bartleman and others weren't moved by the persecution and resistance with which they were met.

What I love about Azusa Street is the intercession of people like Bartleman and Boehmer, but they were only part of the story. Things happened in Topeka, Kansas, that set the stage for Azusa. The Holy Spirit was poured out afresh in 1901 in Topeka with Charles Parham and a group of some people from his Bible school who were seeking the baptism of the Spirit with the evidence of speaking in tongues.

Billy: Agnes Ozman, on January 1, 1901, she was the first one to receive the baptism and speaking in tongues.

Corey: That's right. So, it hits the group meeting in Topeka. Then Parham went and preached in Houston, Texas. Parham stayed in Houston, continuing to conduct revival meetings, and by 1905 he had started another Bible school. A Baptist, African-American man named William J. Seymour, who was blind in one eye, attended an African-American holiness congregation which was pastored by Lucy F. Farrow. She had formerly served as governess in Parham's household. It was Farrow who "arranged for Seymour to attend classes" at Parham's Bible school in Houston; "however, because of the 'Jim Crow' segregation laws of the time, Seymour had to listen to Parham's lectures while sitting apart" from the white students.[8] Seymour heard and accepted Parham's teaching on the baptism of the Holy Spirit.

For a season, Seymour went to the black churches and preached on the baptism while Parham went to the white. But then God moved Seymour to Los Angeles after receiving an invitation to pastor a small congregation there. And up until that time, he had been praying five hours a day for the baptism of the Holy Spirit. And Seymour asked the Lord what He wanted him to do, and basically God said, "Pick it up to seven." See, that is what happens in these seasons. God lays hold of you, and you think, *Man, rough five hours.* But God deepened and increased Seymour's capacity. It wasn't even a month into the Azusa Street outpouring before Seymour began to speak in tongues himself.

But Seymour would become the best-known leader of the Azusa Street revival. As Frank Bartleman said about him, "Brother Seymour generally sat behind two empty shoeboxes, one on top of the other. He usually kept his head inside the top one during the meeting, in prayer. There was no pride there...."[9]

Imagine seeing Seymour with his head in a shoebox, seeking God! That's humility and brokenness right there.

Billy: Seymour didn't start out on Azusa Street. He actually began shepherding a small flock on Bonnie Brae Street. And they were meeting in a house. Though Seymour had been invited initially to pastor another small congregation, the people there had kicked him out because he preached on the baptism of the Holy Spirit, even though as Corey said Seymour hadn't yet received the gift of speaking in tongues. So, Seymour started this other fellowship on Bonnie Brae Street. And the crowds began to gather and grow. The porch of the house there on Bonnie Brae couldn't hold the weight of the number of people gathered on it. And so, they moved the meetings into this abandoned building on Azusa Street.

A one-eyed, African-American man, in the middle of Jim Crow, was used by God to stand in the face of racial injustice in America, and God broke in and poured out His Spirit upon those gathered with him. I can't help but make the obvious connection that God would use a blind man name "See-more" as all part of the testimony of this revival. It's powerful!

Corey: And 656 million believers[10] later—

Billy: I know!

Corey: That three-and-one-half year season tells the story of revival. Bartleman, as an example, said he had to pray for strength simply to complete the walk to the building a few blocks away as he would begin to feel the weight of the manifest presence of God. Furthermore, fire departments received emergency calls from people who said they saw the building on fire. It was a spiritual fire that was evident to the natural eye. That fire of God was there! And Seymour would speak to limbs, and they would grow! Azusa had both the power and the fire of God.

Billy: I can't help but go back to that image of Seymour praying with his head in a shoebox. I mean, just think about that. Evan Roberts would not allow himself to be painted or photographed; in fact, there are very few images of him that have survived because, like Seymour, he did not allow the focus to be upon him.

Picture it. Seymour sat in the front row of this church and put his head in a shoebox and just waited on the Holy Spirit.

You have to read the full story, if you haven't already, in Frank Bartleman's book called *Azusa Street*. And another book

I would encourage you to get is *They Told Me Their Stories* by J. Edward Morris. Morris interviewed all the people who had eyewitness accounts, people who had been at Azusa during the outpouring. Each shared their respective stories with him. There were children during the Azusa Street outpouring who said they played around, playing hide-and-go-seek. The glory cloud would roll into the meeting, and the children said they could run and physically hide amid the smoke of the glory of God. Then there were stories in Morris's book about the number of times people saw an eye form in a socket or an arm just grow back right in front of them. And then there was the miracle of racial unity. Bartleman said, "The 'color line' was washed away in the blood."[11] These were hallmarks of Azusa Street.

Where Wales would have been hallmarked by deep repentance and salvation, Azusa Street was marked by these as well, but Azusa Street was truly hallmarked by the outpouring of Holy Spirit, the baptism of the Holy Spirit with glory, and racial unity. And, as Corey noted, there are now 656 million believers on the earth who have come out of the tributary that was released there in Azusa Street in 1906.

Corey: I love what God did at and through Azusa Street, but I also love what happened at the Hebrides in Scotland in the late 1940s.

Billy: Yeah, we are back over to Europe. So, the Hebrides revival, that's probably my second favorite, and then Cane Ridge would be my third. I mean, Azusa Street is the big deal. You can't negate or minimize its historic impact, but when I think about lesser-known revivals, I think of Wales, Hebrides, and then Cane Ridge.

Anyway, Hebrides was led by a man named Duncan Campbell. It's a fantastic story because the people on the island were already praying. There were these two older intercessors who were sisters in their early eighties. Their names were Peggy and Christine Smith. They were both blind. They conducted prayer meetings and felt compelled to call their pastor to account. They told him that God was coming and admonished their pastor to get right with Him.

This is one of the most bizarre stories. The sisters prayed and heard the Lord say He was going to send Duncan Campbell. They contacted Campbell, asking him to come, but he was already committed to speak at a convocation in England at that time. In fact, it was a huge ministerial convocation. So, Campbell told them *no.* Yet the two sisters believed they had clearly heard from God, so they began making arrangements to print announcements that Campbell was coming. However, they ran into some strong resistance from pastors who said Campbell wasn't coming. The Smith sisters printed the announcements anyway.

Meanwhile, this bigger convocation ended up getting cancelled, and Campbell then went to the Hebrides Island via ship. And when he showed up at the port there, the person who received the boats and ferries asked him as he deboarded the ship, "Are you Duncan Campbell?" After Campbell affirmed that he was, the man said, "We've been expecting you."

Perplexed, Campbell asked, "Well, what do you mean that you have been expecting me? I didn't tell them I was coming. I told them I wasn't coming."

The man replied, "No, no, the Lord told us you were coming."

Shortly thereafter, Duncan Campbell was met by a minister and two others with him. One of them went over to Duncan and looked him in the eye and asked, "Mr. Campbell, can I ask you this question, are you walking with God?"[12]

"Well, I think I can say this, that I fear God."

The man looked at Campbell and said, "Well, if you fear God, that will do."

That will do. And so, what they had already churned up in intercession was burning. And the Lord just used Duncan Campbell as this match to start the thing. And for me, my favorite story is that first meeting. They called this meeting, and people gathered. And it was a good meeting. Nothing out of the ordinary happened. God was there, but it wasn't a revival. They dismissed the meeting, and this young man grabbed Campbell and said, "Wait a minute. The Lord promised He was going to pour out His Spirit." He quoted Isaiah 44:3 to Campbell.

Then the young man started crying out in intercession, "God, You made a promise, to pour water on the thirsty, and floods upon dry ground, and You're not doing it." The young man continued to pray when he went into a frozen-like trance. But a power was released at that young man's intercession.

And that night as Campbell and others were walking out of the meeting, all of the sudden, horses and buggies and people started gathering to the meeting. They had already finished the meeting. It was over, but there was a group now showing up to the church, and they were saying, "We feel drawn to the church right now. That we are to continue to have a meeting." So, they all went back in, and that was the match that ignited the whole thing.

And the story of the Hebrides is so profound because, literally, what was released on the Isle of Lewis, which is the main island where the thing started, was so intense that people turned themselves into the police because they were under the conviction of the Holy Spirit. And they said you could drive in the middle of the night, driving your buggy or whatever, and you would see houses with lights on at two and three in the morning. People were crying out, groaning in intercession, wailing before the Lord as this spirit of travail had come down and taken possession of the whole place.

Corey: Just think about that for a minute. Think about the people where you live. I mean, like within a fifteen-mile radius, turning themselves over to the police. Think about every pedophile ring, every crack house, every domestically violent man, every other arrestable sinner walking to the police station and saying, "Arrest me. I'm guilty."

Duncan was awakened at three in the morning, according to one story. And he walked to a house and saw the people outside their house laying on the hay bales, crying out to God. He then passed the police station, which was packed. And he interviewed one of the guys there, asking him why he was at the station.

"I don't know," the man replied. "All that I know is that everything I've ever done wrong was made known to me. And I knew that I had to turn myself in." That is the John 16:8 spirit of conviction that shines the light on everything done wrong and exposes a person's need for the Savior. And I love that.

I had heard another story about the Hebrides revival that involved a young man who knelt in a meeting and read Psalm 24:3–4,

> *Who may ascend into the hill of the Lord? Or who may stand in His holy place? He who has clean hands and a pure heart, who has not lifted up his soul to an idol, nor sworn deceitfully.*

Shutting His Bible, he then said, "It seems to me just so much humbug. To be praying, as we are praying, to be waiting as we are waiting, if we ourselves are not rightly related to God. Oh, my dear brethren, let's take that to heart."[13] Then he began praying, "God, are my hands clean? Is my heart pure?" According to Campbell,

> That dear man got no further. He fell on his knees, and then on his face among the straw, and within a matter of minutes, three of the elders fell into a trance . . . when that happened in the barn, a power was let loose that shook the whole of Lewis. I say shook Lewis! God stepped

down. The Holy Spirit began to move among
the people....[14]

God moved in that season with deep intercession. See,
I believe in that. I believe in moments like that. I believe in
transactional points where God brings us to such a place of
desperation that it moves beyond good prayer, loud prayer,
and fiery prayer. It moves into a divine transaction because of
the depth of hunger and desperation that pulls something out
of God.

God's not doing things automatically or mechanically
when it comes to revival. No, when God pours out His Spirit,
when He sends revival, something transactional is taking
place. It has to do with hunger. And we will talk about that
later. But I want to highlight here that hunger pulls something
out of God that may have been reserved for another time.

Billy: And He definitely moves in response to the desire of a
heart that says it wants Him more than anything. And we see
that in every one of these stories.

Corey: The famous prayer of the Hebrides is Isaiah 64:

> *Oh, that You would rend the heavens! That You
> would come down! That the mountains might shake
> at Your presence—as fire burns brushwood, as fire
> causes water to boil—to make Your name known to
> Your adversaries, that the nations may tremble at
> Your presence! When You did awesome things for
> which we did not look, You came down, the moun-
> tains shook at Your presence.* (vv. 1–3)

This passage rocks my heart today. I'm provoked to pray for the *Oh* of Isaiah 64. We need the *Oh* to stir us into intercession. And we need the *Please* of Moses from Exodus 33:18—*"Please, show me Your glory!"* A depth of desperation, a depth hunger, a depth of humility, and a depth of need we must express to God are in that *Please* and in that *Oh*. We need God to birth all of that in us.

When we have the *Please* and the *Oh*, our prayers become divine transactions that pull on something from God that can alter the trajectory of the lives of many. We need the kind of encounters we've been talking about so that we're never the same. We need transactional prayers in this hour. *Mark us with this, I pray, Jesus.*

NOTES

1. Roberts Liardon, *God's Generals: Evan Roberts* (New Kensington, PA: Whitaker House, 1996, 2012), 14.

2. W.T. Stead, "What I saw in Wales," in *The Revival in the West*, The Welsh Revival, http://www.welshrevival.org/histories/stead1/03.htm/.

3. E. Cynolwyn Pugh, "The Welsh Revival of 1904–1905," *Theology Today* 12.2 (1955): 227.

4. Frank Bartleman, *Azusa Street: An Eyewitness Account to the Birth of the Pentecostal Revival* (New Kensington, PA: Whitaker House, 1982), 8.

5. Bartleman, *Azusa Street*, 31.

6. Pandita Ramabai, *The Great Mukti Revival* (1906), Digital Showcase: Holy Spirit Research Center, https://digitalshowcase.oru.edu/hsbooks/9/.

7. Frank Bartleman, *How Pentecost Came to Los Angeles*, (Los Angeles: F. Bartleman, 1925), 37.

8. Gary B. McGee, "William J. Seymour and the Azusa Street Revival," Features section of AG.org, April 4, 1999, https://news.ag.org/en/features/william-j-seymour-and-the-azusa-street-revival/.

9. Frank Bartleman, *Azusa Street* (South Plainfield, NJ: Bridge Publishing, 1980), 58.

10. Gina A. Zurlo, Todd M. Johnson, Peter F. Crossing, "World Christianity and Mission 2021: Questions about the Future." *International Bulletin of Mission Research* 46.1 (January 1, 2022): 18.

11. Bartleman, *How Pentecost Came to Los Angeles*, 54.

12. Duncan Campbell, "When God Stepped Down," OChristian.com, http://articles.ochristian.com/article13382.shtml/.

13. Campbell, "When God Stepped Down."

14. Campbell, "When God Stepped Down."

10

Historic Great Awakenings

We want to look back a little further in America's history to the two Great Awakenings, which were marked by regions coming underneath the manifest presence of God. The hallmarks of these two awakenings were deep conviction of sin, deep repentance, and many salvations. Revisiting these seasons when God moved mightily upon the frontier landscape of America encourages us today. It stirs faith in our hearts to believe that God can do it again.

Corey: The First Great Awakening occurred between the 1730s and 1750s. Men like Jonathan Edwards, George Whitefield, and John Wesley were among the many used to call

America to repentance. It was an explosive time as America was moving toward becoming a sovereign nation no longer under the oversight of a monarch. There were wars during that time, and I want to connect the timing of revival in context to wars and judgment events. Why? Because I believe that the Lord is coming in with force of salvation, power, preaching, and fury to reap a harvest to protect for the coming hour. And He's protecting souls for eternity because He knows what's coming upon a nation and what the nation is reaping. Judgment is coming, and there will be a great shaking.

When I think about revival, I think about what we discussed earlier: When God comes, God comes. And there is creation's groan. There is crisis. There is the sin of man. There are the judgments of God and the outpouring of the Spirit. When Heaven gets closer, all the stuff in normal time now begins to manifest; everything comes alive. And I think of all these agents being involved during the First Great Awakening.

Billy: When we're talking about revival versus the divine activity of the divine Heaven unleashed, we're not talking about some sort of triumphalism where everything is perfect. And one of the things that I think is probably a challenge for us Charismatic Christians is that we just want everything to be blessed and awesome and good, especially in areas of our temporal comforts. And the Father really doesn't care about our temporal comforts like we do. He cares about the glory of His Son. And this triumphalism, where we think we will win and enjoy the benefits of that win, is not legitimate at all. It's more sugar high and a pep-rally kind of thing to hype people up. But when we actually read the biblical narrative and see what happened in the First Great Awakening, it's like what Corey is saying as revival often comes in as a mercy stroke right before a time of judgment.

Corey: That's exactly right. And so, we see in the 1700s in America that God sends these brothers from England, John and Charles Wesley. John Wesley came to America and toiled as a missionary; however, his missionary work proved unsuccessful. So, he returned to England.

Billy: And he met the Moravians on his return to England. The Moravians were going on missions trips, and they were packing all of their belongings in their caskets. They were using their caskets as their luggage! And John Wesley saw these Moravians and was convicted.

Corey: Yes, basically, Wesley was returning to England on a ship when the ship ran into a great storm. And Wesley, the missionary minister, watched in amazement as this group of Moravians sang songs and appeared to be completely at rest at the threat of eminent death. And it began to deeply convict him of the fact that he was not secure about his eternal state and he feared death. The Moravians survived the journey, but Wesley was depressed. As he wrote, "I who went to America to convert others was never myself converted to God."[1]

After arriving back in England, he felt defeated by his failure in America, and so he looked to the Moravians. And that is what led John Wesley to a man named Peter Boehler, a young Moravian missionary waiting to go to Georgia himself. Boehler began to talk to Wesley about grace and righteousness and faith.

On May 24, 1738, John Wesley went to a meeting on Aldersgate Street in London. There he heard the reading of the preface of Martin Luther's Epistle to the Romans. This led to his encounter when his "heart was strangely warmed."[2] Something significant happened there. It gave him the assurance of faith he had been lacking. Whether his experience was a full conversion, a baptism in the Spirit, or something similar, all we know is something happened that turned this man into a lightning rod who changed the course of history. He later came back to America, and he began to minister like an apostle.

Billy: Also prior to his conversion, John and Charles Wesley and George Whitefield were "members of a religious society at Oxford University called the Holy Club and 'Methodists' due to their methodical piety and rigorous asceticism."[3] All three would end up ministering in America.

The Methodist circuit riders took the spirit of revival that Wesley was carrying and shared it everywhere. And the thing that John Wesley and the circuit riders had was a tireless determination to preach the gospel until all would hear. They really had the sense that they were going to bring the gospel to everybody, and the Lord met them with signs, wonders, and dramatic happenings. As a matter of fact, the Wesley brothers' journals read like some Charismatic or Pentecostal writings even though they didn't speak in tongues. They recounted dramatic things like healings and people falling out under the power of the Holy Spirit. And John Wesley was a significant figure that was breathing revival fire while Charles Wesley was writing the great hymns of the Faith.

Corey: George Whitefield was another lightning rod. Microphones, of course, didn't exist in his day. It was said that you could hear Whitefield's voice from a mile away. I mean that was supernatural. These guys didn't just do a once-a-week meeting. Men like Whitefield preached six times a day. He would preach at five in the morning to the miners going out. Then he would preach at seven o'clock, at nine o'clock, at noon, and at three in the afternoon—every day!

Billy: Can you imagine the hunger in people who would go that many times to hear preaching? And Whitefield, when you read about him, you find his story is compelling. He was kicked out of this church, kicked out of that church, and kicked out of another church. He showed up at a graveyard one Saturday, and 10,000 people gathered to hear the gospel. And 2,500 of them were converted!

Corey: The power of conviction would rest on Whitefield's meetings. People came face to face with their eternal fate as he preached. "Some people even fell to the floor as though dead, so strong were their feelings of conviction when they heard Whitefield's messages."[4] He was such an incredible orator that his description of a storm at sea "was so vivid that a sailor in the audience actually cried out, 'To the lifeboats! To the lifeboats!'"[5]

Whitefield died at fifty. To him, it was all about fulfilling the will of God. And for that man, it was to burn, and in a good way, he burned out. He just completely gave himself. John Wesley, on the other hand, kept going for so many decades and much longer than Whitefield, as Wesley lived into his eighties.

Jonathan Edwards was a Congregational minister in Massachusetts. His "Sinners in the Hands of an Angry God" brought such a spirit of conviction that people would dig their fingers into the pews, leaving marks in the wood. Forces would pick people up and throw them to the front of the room.

Billy: And perhaps the biggest testimony from "Sinners in the Hands of an Angry God" was the open vision people experienced where the floor beneath them disappeared and they seemed to see the very flames of hell.

When we talk about revival preachers, what we see is that they didn't mince words about eternal judgment. They expressed the grace and the love of God, but they also declared the reality that so many are unwilling to touch today—that, without Jesus, there is eternal judgment. Without Jesus, there is separation from God in the lake of fire.

Francis Chan wrote a book called *Erasing Hell* because, in the last decade, it's become in vogue to decide, well, hell isn't real, and everybody goes to Heaven. Or hell is a momentary thing. And Francis Chan, after writing a book on love, wrote this book on hell to describe the apostolic truths in the New Testament—that hell is forever and there is eternal torment there.

And here's the point, in revival preaching when we talk about conviction of sin, it's not just, "Oh, I feel bad because of the sin." No, in revival preaching, people recognize that, without Jesus' grace saving them, they will spend an eternity in hell. And this life is not a game. Revival preaching causes its hearers who have become all too familiar with church and

God suddenly to become sobered by the reality of hell and their not living in a way that pleases God.

We have to live a life of love, grace, and mercy. But we cannot and should not think that we can live in whatever manner we want to live or live in outright disobedience to God without suffering repercussions. And the painful reality is that, without God, we will be eternally separated from Him. And these ministers all preached that. They confronted their listeners and blew these things up in these mass revivals, and they all preached the reality of eternal damnation without Jesus.

Corey: I don't think it's going to be anything different than what the Lord is going to do at the end of the age. In Revelation 14:6–11, the proclamations of the three angels tell us what we need to do and what will happen to those who walk in the fear of the Lord and worship Him and to those who don't:

> *Then I saw another angel flying in the midst of heaven, having the everlasting gospel to preach to those who dwell on the earth—to every nation, tribe, tongue, and people—saying with a loud voice, "Fear God and give glory to Him, for the hour of His judgment has come; and worship Him who made heaven and earth, the sea and springs of water." And another angel followed saying, "Babylon is fallen, is fallen, that great city, because she has made all nations drink of the wine of the wrath of her fornication." Then a third angel followed them, saying with a loud voice, "If anyone*

worships the beast and his image, and receives his mark on his forehead or on his hand, he himself shall also drink of the wine of the wrath of God, which is poured out full strength into the cup of His indignation. He shall be tormented with fire and brimstone in the presence of the holy angels and in the presence of the Lamb. And the smoke of their torment ascends forever and ever; and they have no rest day or night, who worship the beast and his image, and whoever receives the mark of his name."

And something we want to talk about, apostolic preachers, revival preachers, like Wesley, Whitefield, and Edwards operated in deep conviction that pierced through the hearts of their hearers. It's the greatest message. But outside of it, it is terrible. The wrath of God is coming. Romans 1:16–32 talks about the torment of eternal destruction and our revealing the glorious gift that God has given us in Christ and presenting that to a generation.

Billy: Out of gratitude and deep love, we should share the gospel of Christ to rescue souls from that place of eternal torment.

Corey: Yes, exactly. So that is going to come back in our revival preaching. Whether we realize it or not, conviction-inspiring preaching demonstrates and expresses the love of God and the gift of God. We quote John 3:16, *"For God so loved the world that He gave His only begotten son, that whoever believes in Him should not perish but have everlasting life."* That's the great gift—the love of God expressed through His Son, providing believers with eternal life. But then in a couple verses later, Jesus said: "*And this is the condemnation, that the light has come into the world, and men loved darkness rather than light, because their deeds were evil*" (John 3:19). Revival preaching has to present the gift while warning of the fallout of our rejecting the gift.

Another preacher I want to mention was David Brainerd, who was preaching among Indigenous people during the First Great Awakening. And as he would proclaim the goodness and love of God, those listening felt unworthy to come to such a kind Savior. His preaching on God's love brought intense conviction.

Before the Revolutionary War, God brought the First Great Awakening, and He brought the Second Great Awakening in the years prior to the Civil War.

Billy: And one of my favorite revival stories is in that Second Great Awakening group. It's the Cane Ridge revival that happened in 1801 in Cane Ridge, Kentucky. You can go to the Cane Ridge Revival Campground today. And they have some of the original facilities out there. My family and I went there. I remember walking around the grounds, overwhelmed by what I learned had taken place there.

Barton Stone, a Presbyterian minister, was one of the chief figures. The church he pastored "decided to invite other local Presbyterian and Methodist churches to participate in its annual Communion service. Ministers from Presbyterian, Methodist, and Baptist backgrounds participated."[6] The Presbyterians had a tradition of such joint communion gatherings. People came in August of 1801 to Cane Ridge Meeting House in Kentucky, intending on making camp and joining "a vibrant worship experience."[7] And "as many as 20,000 to 30,000 people gathered" in this wilderness place in Kentucky.[8] And literally, even to this day, when you drive out there, you can begin to think you're lost because it seems to be in the middle of nowhere.

Well, the great throng of people showed up, and there were no facilities with running water like we have today. No conveniences or comforts were made available to any of those in attendance, but those who came had a hunger burning in their hearts as they wanted to meet with God.

This revival continued for a period of weeks where thousands were coming and going at all times. Here's what happened. Without any means for amplification or a platform high enough for tens of thousands to see or hear the speakers, Stone and the leaders decided to have multiple preachers preaching at various locations throughout the camp. Several preachers would speak at once. Perhaps one minister would preach from a stump with a few hundred around him. Another would speak from a cart or wagon to his few hundred or more closest to him. And all these different ministers were preaching at the same time. Can you picture it? And the same power of God that was being released in one spot was being released throughout the camp. Just as the preaching of the Word was going forth, the Lord was moving upon the people with power.

One of the hallmarks of the Cane Ridge revival is that the Holy Spirit would grip people with unusual manifestations. Peter Cartwright gave the following report:

Just in the midst of our controversies on the subject of this powerful exercises among the people under preaching, a new exercise broke out among us, called the jerks, which was overwhelming in its effects upon the bodies and minds of the people. No matter whether they were saints or sinners, they would be taken under a warm song or sermon, and seized with a convulsive jerking all over, which they could not by any possibility avoid, and the more they resisted, the more they jerked....

To see those proud young gentlemen and young ladies, dressed in their silks, jewelry, and prunella, from top to toe, take the jerks would often excite my risibilities [sic]. The first jerk or so, you would see their fine bonnets, caps, and combs fly; and so sudden would be the jerking of the head that their long loose hair would crack almost as loud as a wagoner's whip.[9]

The seizing power of the Holy Spirit gripped and delivered people. And it was the force of Heaven coming to bear on human flesh. What will give way in such happenings is human flesh.

The autobiography of James Finley contains his personal experience at Cane Ridge. He described his arrival upon the grounds like this:

Here a scene presented itself to my mind not only novel and unaccountable, but awful beyond description. A vast crowd, supposed by some to have amounted to twenty-five thousand, was collected together. The noise was like the roar of Niagara. The vast sea of human beings seemed to be agitated as if by a storm. I counted seven ministers, all preaching at one time, some on stumps, others in wagons.... Some of the people were singing, others praying, some crying for mercy in the most piteous accents, while others were shouting most vociferously. While witnessing these scenes, a peculiarly-strange sensation, such as I had never felt before, came over me. My heart beat tumultuously, my knees trembled, my lip quivered, and I felt as though I must fall to the ground.[10]

Finley soon retired to the woods, overwhelmed by his experience. And when he later returned, he said,

I returned to the scene of excitement the waves of which, if possible, had risen still higher. The same awfulness of feeling came over me. I stepped up on a log, where I could have a better view of the surging sea of humanity. The scene that then presented itself to my mind was indescribable. At one time I saw at least five hundred swept down in a moment, as if a battery of a thousand guns had been opened upon them, and then immediately followed shrieks and shouts that rent the very heavens. My hair rose up on my head, my whole frame trembled, the blood ran cold in my veins, and I fled for the woods a second time, and wished I had stayed at home. While I remained here my feelings became intense and insupportable. A sense of suffocation and blindness seemed to come over me, and I thought I was going to die.[11]

Just at the preaching of the Word, people were going down under the power of God. This didn't happen via the typical act of people laying hands on individuals as we see in modern Charismatic churches. This was at the preaching of the Word! The Holy Spirit was rushing on people, and they were being slain under the force of the power of the Word of God.

Can you imagine experiencing what Finley and others experienced as the power of God came down upon a mass of people? I mean, just think about this for a minute. The fear of the Lord was intense. People physically got up, not because they were offended, but felt like they had to get away, even running away because of the fear of the Lord. The recognition of the reality of God was so stark that they were literally running in fear and terror. And the Holy Spirit swept down upon them—He didn't let up!

Corey: It was like a hurricane or a wave that was overtaking them all.

Billy: So, Cane Ridge sparked multiple denominations out of its movement. And that revival, that 1801 revival, was one of the very first sparks of the Second Great Awakening.

Corey: I heard that those at Cane Ridge would chop the trees down so that people would hang onto them when those waves would come through. They would have to hold on. The deep spirit of conviction was evident in the testimonies. I've heard it said there are counties today in Kentucky that are still dry because of the power of God that hit Cane Ridge. There were alcoholic counties that became dry counties to this day because of the touch of God that came down.

Billy: When I walked around the campground there a couple of years ago, I was just imagining the twenty or thirty thousand in mass and the days of visitation. I wanted to get a picture of what that looked like. When I was there, I had a moment with the Lord. With tears streaming down my face, I asked, "God, will You do this in America again? Will You do this in America again?"

And I won't say that I had a word of the Lord or anything, but I noted a sense in my soul that He is going to do it again! *Jesus, so be it!*

Corey: So, that was in the early 1800s. Then there was a lawyer in Upstate New York, and his name was Charles Finney. Long story short, Finney began having encounters with the Lord. His famous one was when he was at his law office, and the presence of God began to come on him in a powerful way.

> The 29-year-old lawyer Charles Grandison Finney had decided he must settle the question of his soul's salvation. So on October 10, 1821, he headed out into the woods near his Adams, New York, home to find God. "I will give my

heart to God, or I never will come down from there," he said. After several hours, he returned to his office, where he experienced such forceful emotion that he questioned those who could not testify to a similar encounter.

"The Holy Spirit...seemed to go through me, body and soul," he later wrote. "I could feel the impression, like a wave of electricity, going through and through me. Indeed it seemed to come in waves of liquid love, for I could not express it any other way."[12]

Finney experienced that baptism of fire, God gripped him, and God possessed him. And the short of the story is that the Lord used this man in a mighty way.

And I just want to say to you, God uses people. God puts His hands on real human beings. I believe He is going to release His anointing on whole companies worldwide. God is into taking His hands, putting them on men and on women, and using these people for a season. For a twenty-year season in Upstate New York, the power of God operated through Finney's life in an unparalleled way. The tangible, regional spirit of conviction, the conscious spirit of conviction that came upon people was exceptional in the fact that Finney would be on boats or on trains and arrive in a city for a short, thirty-minute stop, when souls would fall under this spirit of conviction. It would break out. God would move into that city or that region, and souls in great number would get saved.

My favorite Charles Finney story was when he went to Utica, New York:

Finney seemed so anointed with the Holy Spirit that people were often brought under conviction of sin just by looking at him. When holding meetings at Utica, New York, he visited a large factory and was looking at the machinery. At the sight of him one of the operatives, and then another, and then another broke down and wept under a sense of their sins, and finally so many were sobbing and weeping that the machinery had to be stopped while Finney pointed them to Christ.[13]

If you have seen any pictures of Finney, you could understand how these people could fall under such conviction because those eyes would get you. When I look at a picture of him two-hundred year later, his eyes terrify me. And so, Finney stared at machinery, and people got convicted. They were weeping and groaning when, finally, Finney delivered the Word of God with power and glory.

New York during Finney's ministry was in the heat of revival. Some of the estimates in that period say they saw 500,000 souls, new converts, come to the Lord in a matter of two months. That just blows my mind!

This is my favorite part of the Finney story. It involves a man by the name of Daniel Nash. From 1824 to 1831, he interceded for Finney. Prior to his connection to Finney, Nash had pastored a couple of times. He became ill, but he had seen revival come to his church. But then the church voted him out. He was in his early forties, yet they voted him out because they deemed him too old.

Then Nash came into this season where he had something wrong with his eyes. And he was like shut up, shut down in his house for a long, long time with this illness of his eyes. And something happened in that season. And he came into something in God in the ministry of prayer and intercession. It was after that, for a seven-year period, Daniel Nash and another guy by the name of Abel Clary began to understand a principle of battling in the heavenlies in intercession for effective evangelism. These men would win the battle in the heavenlies so that, when Finney would come to town, the Word of God would go forth in power and have great effect.

Finney recounted that he had seen Daniel Nash at an event and had heard him pray. Finney had even heard Nash be able to discern the spiritual condition of different people.

> If you ask Charles Finney, he will point to one man who partnered with him in his crusades: Daniel Nash. Daniel Nash joined himself to Finney for the purpose of prayer. When Finney was invited to speak in a city, Nash would arrive three or four weeks early, rent a room, find a small group of like-minded Christians to join him, and start a prayer meeting to plead with God for souls. Once the public meetings began, Nash usually did not attend. He and his group would stay hidden away, agonizing in prayer for the conviction of the Holy Spirit to melt the crowd.[14]

Once, Nash rented a basement in order for them to intercede for revival and souls.

> On one occasion, Finney himself noted in his journal that when he arrived in a particular town for a revival, he was met by a lady who ran a boarding house. "Brother Finney," she asked, "do you know Mr. Nash? He and two other men have been at my boarding house for the last three days, but they haven't eaten a bite of food. They have been this way for three days, lying prostrate on the floor and groaning. I thought something awful must have happened to them. I was afraid to go in, and I didn't know what to do. Would you please come and see about them?" And Charles Finney replied, "No, it isn't necessary. They just have a spirit of travail in prayer."[15]

Nash, this hidden intercessor, and the power between intercession and evangelism gripped my life. So, my wife and I named our son *Josiah Nash*. We called him *Nash*.

Billy: And I have a Josiah.

Corey: Yeah, I love it. But let me say this. You may have children. I would encourage you to name them, prophesy over them, and declare who they are. We named our son Nash. And he was with us for nine and a half months, and then he went home to be with the Lord. But in so many ways, I feel like he is my hidden intercessor. And I feel like we're in ministry together to this day. And honestly, I feel like God has put a vision in my heart for hundreds of thousands, and even millions, of what I am calling *Nasharites*. It's the Nasharite army of intercessors that are going to break open regions for a new church planting movement, evangelism, missions, and I think these are going to be at the core of what God's going to be doing.

I believe God's setting up houses of prayer, funded and released across the earth. As a generation is getting rid of stages and platforms, and beginning to understand the glory and the power they have before the stage and the audience of Heaven, I am asking God to release that Nasharite grace, that He would raise up Nasharites all over the earth, intercessors for revival. We want to see the spirit of intercession for revival lay hold of men and women, young and old. *We believe, God, that You will release Your fire and grace.*

Billy: If you think this might even be you right now, I want you to put your hand on your heart and pray with me.

> *Father, in the name of Jesus Christ, mark every person that's responding right now. Give them the vision of what Daniel Nash laid hold of, of what intercessors of old like Peggy and Christine Smith laid hold of, of what Bartleman laid hold of. God, that many, thousands upon thousands of this generation, would be gripped by what the Holy Spirit has gripped them for. That they would learn what it means to travail until souls are birthed. That they would learn what it means to win the*

war in the heavenlies. God, I am asking You to grip hearts that they wouldn't walk away from it. And even now, release fire on their hearts. That they wouldn't be able to step out of it. I pray for travail that births souls. The very graces that you released to Nash, to the Smiths, God, the grace that you released to Bartleman and Roberts and so many others over the years. I'm asking, God, release it on an entire generation of intercessors. I'm asking You, God, for twenty-year-olds to get a vision of what it can look like not to care one thing about what a human audience thinks, but that they would have an audience before Your throne. Do it, we ask, Lord, in the name of Jesus. Thank You, Lord.

NOTES

1. "First Great Awakening," Wikipedia, https://en.wikipedia.org/wiki/First_Great_Awakening/.

2. "First Great Awakening," Wikipedia.

3. "First Great Awakening," Wikipedia.

4. "Controversial George Whitefield," Christianity.com, April 28, timeline/1701-1800/controversial-george-whitefield-11630198.html/.

5. "Controversial George Whitefield," Christianity.com.

6. "Cane Ridge Revival, Wikipedia, https://en.wikipedia.org/wiki/Cane_Ridge_Revival/.

7. "Religion on America's Western Front," caneridge.org, https://www.caneridge.org/.

8. "Religion on America's Western Front," caneridge.org.

9. Peter Cartwright, *Autobiography of Peter Cartwright, The Backwoods Preachers*, edited by W.P. Strickland (New York: Carlton Porter, 1856), 30–31, 34–38, 45–52.

10. "A testimony from the Cane Ridge Revival, 1801," Sermon Index, 2019 post by twayneb, https://www.sermonindex.net/modules/newbb/viewtopic.php?topic_id=30740&forum=40/.

11. "A testimony from the Cane Ridge Revival, 1801," Sermon Index.

12. "Charles Finney: Father of American revivalism," Christianity Today, https://www.christianitytoday.com/history/people/evangelistsandapologists/charles-finney.html/.

13. J. Gilchrist Lawson, *Deeper Experiences of Famous Christians*, (Anderson, IN: Warner Press, 2007), 109–116.

14. "Charles Finney And Daniel Nash," Sermon Central, contributed on May 5, 2012, https://www.sermoncentral.com/sermon-illustrations/81357/charles-finney-and-daniel-nash-evangelism-and-by-sermon-central

15. "Charles Finney And Daniel Nash," Sermon Central.

11

Humility Required

Reading stories of past revivals inspires us. It causes the embers of our desire for God to burst into flames in our hearts. And that's great! We need stories to reignite our believing and contending for revival. But exactly what is it that attracts God? We know He desires to dwell with us, but is there something else that draws Him to us, something that draws on Him to come and invade a city or a region?

We see it in biblical and historical accounts of revival. There is a quality of heart that is a magnet for Heaven's inbreaking. There is a posture or character that calls Heaven down and arrests God's gaze. What is it? Humility.

God is allured by humility arguably more than anything else. And when He draws near to meet humility, the outcomes can be historic. There are many seasons that His response to a humble heart, a humble cry, and a humble prayer has been revival.

Billy: There is a lifestyle necessary to see revival start, to see it broken open. By the grace of God, we operate in accordance with what the Scripture says: *"God resists the proud, but gives grace to the humble"* (James 4:6). We who are hungry for Him are compelled to humble ourselves before Him. This is not about trying to leverage God; in fact, we can't leverage God, but we can touch something in Him with our lifestyle—with our prayers, our hearts, and our love—that moves Him to act in power on our behalf.

Isaiah 57:15 says:

> *For thus says the High and Lofty One who inhabits eternity, whose name is Holy: "I dwell in the high and holy place, with him who has a contrite and humble spirit, to revive the spirit of the humble, and to revive the heart of the contrite ones."*

Think about what God is saying here. He is the High and Lofty One, which means He is above all. He dwells somewhere high and holy. He inhabits eternity. Then God says He dwells there with someone—someone who is contrite and humble or poor in spirit. And He dwells with the humble to revive their spirit. In Isaiah 57:15, God connects His dwelling with us with Him initiating revival. And He specifically narrows His dwelling and reviving to a certain people—those who are humble.

None of us is born humble. Quite the opposite, we are hardwired with pride. Pride was the seminal sin of lucifer, and it became part of our DNA after the fall. But Scripture promises us, *"God resists the proud, but gives grace to the humble"* (James 4:6; 1 Pet. 5:5). It's when we choose to humble ourselves that the divine ability (grace) is poured into our lives. And what is revival but days of multiplied grace upon the people of God.

Corey: Another verse that has gripped me to prepare for God's invasion is Isaiah 66:1–2:

> *"Heaven is My throne, and earth is My footstool. Where is the house that you will build Me? And where is the place of My rest? For all those things My hand has made, and all those things exist," says the Lord. "But on this one will I look: On him who is poor and of a contrite spirit, and who trembles at My word."*

Do you want to grab God's attention? Do you want to stick out of the crowd?

He is sitting in Heaven and resting His feet on the earth. He is surrounded by billions of angels singing His praise and glory incessantly, and yet He looks at you and me and declares, "I want you to build Me something, and I want to rest in you and upon you." Three distinct realities draw God's manifest presence to come and dwell: poverty of spirit, contrition of spirit, and a trembling heart before the Word of God.

I believe these three graces are what the Holy Spirit is screaming to the Church in this hour. We boast in our strength, our numbers, our attractive churches with our beautiful displays and services and worship leaders and preachers, yet these aren't what gets His attention. Humility and poverty, they get His attention.

Church has never been more beautiful and excellent in our presentation, yet it's never been so absent of the manifest fear and glory of God. We must ask, "Why?"

Jesus came out of the forty-day fasting season as a Man on fire. He immediately began to go to the synagogues in Galilee and preached the gospel of the Kingdom. He healed the sick, delivered the oppressed, and for every person set free, ten more would show up. Jesus used the miracles, healings, and deliverances to draw the large crowds, and as they assembled, He went up on a mountain, His disciples came to Him, and then He opened His mouth and would release His first public message: the Sermon on the Mount.

Jesus had just manifested the Kingdom of God and preached the gospel of the Kingdom, but now He was going to instruct the people on how to build a house internally and corporately to host and steward the Kingdom. The first word out of His mouth was the word, "Blessed." He was about to flip everyone's understanding of happiness, greatness, and success:

> *Blessed are the poor in spirit, for theirs is the kingdom of heaven. Blessed are those who mourn, for they shall be comforted. Blessed are the meek, for they shall inherit the earth. Blessed are those who hunger and thirst for righteousness, for they shall be filled. Blessed are the merciful, for they shall obtain mercy. Blessed are the pure in heart, for they shall see God. Blessed are the peacemakers, for they shall be called the sons of God. Blessed are those who are persecuted*

for righteousness' sake, for theirs is the kingdom of heaven. Blessed are you when they revile and perse-cute you, and say all kinds of evil against you falsely for My sake. Rejoice and be exceedingly glad, for great is your reward in heaven, for so they perse-cuted the prophets who were before you. (Matthew 5:3–12)

Jesus confronted the spirit of the age and the kingdoms of the world by this message. He emphatically declared that greatness in the Kingdom of Heaven looks like weakness in the kingdoms of this world.

The Holy Spirit is going to see to it that His people look like Jesus and are transformed and conformed into His image. The meekness and lowliness of heart of our King will become reality in His Bride.

Billy: We must be humble. And this means we must humble ourselves. We have the challenge from Jesus and from both James and Peter to humble ourselves. So, there is this critical application of the grace of God by which we don't allow our-selves to be "in it" for ourselves. When we live with a "what am I going to get out of this" mentality, we have made self the center. And when self is the center, pride is the motivator. Humility says, "I want your desires and longings to be served over any of my desires and longings." When we move from being in it for our dream, ministry, persona, or platform to being in it fully for His dream, greatness, glory, and grandeur, days of revival are at the door.

* my experience w/ travail/
humility came 1st   RECLAIMING REVIVAL
then outpouring of spirit

When Jesus said, *"Blessed are the poor in spirit,"* He was talking about our coming to a recognition that we are nothing, we have nothing, and we can do nothing without Him (Matt. 5:3). As long as we think we are bringing something to the table or adding something to the equation, we are not poor in spirit. ✗ /// /

Recently, the Lord visited our leadership team in a very personal and powerful way. He was touching our hearts and causing us to address areas of false humility and arrogance. He put His finger upon the places where we thought we could do things in our own strength and see them have some sort of Kingdom effect. It was as if He were saying, "You think you are bringing something to the table. But you're not." I was puzzled because I really believed I was trusting Him for everything. Then the Lord put His finger right on it, "Even if you believe you are bringing 10 percent and I'm adding the other 90, you're actually in pride. I bring 100 percent! You bring nothing. I bring grace, and all you can do is say, 'Yes.'" I was undone and shocked by my own false humility. My belief that I was bringing something to the table was the very thing that God was highlighting as an area of pride.

It's the picture of Peter and some of the disciples fishing all night and not catching one fish in their own strength (see John 21). These guys were skilled fishermen who had lived their lives catching fish. It's what they did. But after struggling all night, they had nothing to show for it. And when Jesus came and told them to *"cast the net on the right side of the boat,"* they humbled themselves and obeyed the Master and caught 153 fish (John 21:6, 11). Their all-night fishing in their

* but i do have to bring Smth. So what does lance?

*preparation, study, obedience, willingness,
time of seeking 130 etc... ?

own strength resulted in nothing. Their one cast under the direction and grace of Jesus resulted in catching 153 fish.

We must get this revelation: When we are in the grace of God, in humility, versus when we are in the flesh, the score will always be 153 to nothing!

Corey: It's truly our "nothingness" that moves God. When we live deeply aware that we bring nothing to the table but our need of Him, we can be confident that He will respond and move in our midst. I believe the Lord is driving this point home in this season both individually and corporately.

We've referenced the day of Pentecost several times in this book, but we really need to lock in on what those disciples were doing for those ten days preceding the day of Pentecost. They were gathering, praying, and seeking God together. They were following the prophet Joel's prescription of how to respond in hours of crisis: *"Turn to Me with all your heart, with fasting, with weeping, and with mourning"* (Joel 2:12). Then Joel declared,

> *Blow the trumpet in Zion, consecrate a fast, call a sacred assembly; gather the people, sanctify the congregation, assemble the elders, gather the children and the nursing babes; let the bridegroom go out from his chamber, and the bride from her dressing room. Let the priests, who minister to the Lord, weep between the porch and the altar; let them say, "Spare Your people, O Lord, and do not give Your heritage to reproach, that the nations should rule over them."* (Joel 2:15–17)

Joel's prescription is profoundly simple. It's so simple that anyone can do it, but it's so simple, few do it. The prescription is this: "Go low. Humble yourself. Turn to God and humble yourself with others." I believe wholeheartedly that we will see a mass revival touch our nation if we connect with the fact that corporate humility releases a corporate move of God.

Billy: When I was a young minister, I couldn't help but want to be on every platform. I was hungry and passionate for God, yet full of attitude. In our youthfulness, we can be amped up in our own gifts and strength. That was me. I wanted every platform, every microphone, every opportunity to minister. Then I would notice others in ministry who were operating in tremendous anointings, offering the grace of God in powerful ways, and yet they were humble. It made me wonder how they were staying humble with such dynamic ministries.

For me to be humble, the Lord had to humble me. The Lord had to take me through seasons of crushing to show me that my abilities, my strengths, and my very belief of what I thought I could produce were all nothing. He has had to show me that I could work for Him in my own capabilities and power, and though men might be impressed, ultimately, I would fail. But if I would come under His yoke, where He provides everything, and I learn of Him, then I could step into His grace. And that is the point. God gives grace to the humble. I had to recognize that, without God's enabling power, I didn't have anything to offer. I had to understand and believe that whatever came out of me that was good, anointed, helpful, or impactful for the Kingdom was because of Jesus, not because of me. And I must continue to live in the light of that.

Corey: Humility is what catches God's attention. God answers our prayer for revival by making us humble. God will use a thousand different storylines to bring us to the same destination: humility. When God gets a man or a woman alone, with no confidence in their abilities, wisdom, or resources and brings forth a deep cry for Him, just know that he or she is being prepared to be a vessel for revival.

Billy: If ultimately you are pursuing Him for Him, you will bump into Him. I remember hearing a preacher say, "A lot of you are pursuing God for souls or revival. That would be like a man coming into his home and starting to scream to his wife, 'I want babies! Give me babies!' But did you say *hello* yet? Did you look into your wife's eyes yet? Did you ask how her day went? A lot of times we treat the Lord like that, 'I want fruitfulness. I want revival!' And He's like, 'You didn't even talk to *Me* yet.'"

So, that is the shift we need to make. We want to pursue God for God rather than pursue Him for His outcomes. At some point, I discovered I was more committed to the ends that I thought God was after than I was to God. Getting clarity about where my heart was and what my motivations were broke me. I had sought God for revival for my own ends. I was under the delusion that, if He came in revival, it would make me great. John the Baptist was clear: Jesus must increase, and we *must* decrease (see John 3:30). We don't get to increase when He increases. He increases, and we decrease. If we're seeking Him for our desires, we're missing the point.

When we seek Him for Him, we begin to see Him and get to know who He really is. We begin to experience who He really is as well. We will discover what His being eternal and omnipotent means. He is the transcendent One who knows the end from the beginning. Hang around God for a while and let Him reveal His divine attributes, and suddenly, you become aware of how small you are and how big He is. He begins to tower in your understanding. That's what happened to me. Revelation or knowledge of God gave me a proper perspective of who He is and who I really am, and then the wonder of His love for me started to soar.

When I was a young man, I thought I knew everything there was to know about God, but God blew up my understanding by just revealing a little bit more of Himself to me. I think of Job when he finally got a revelation of God. He said,

> *I have heard of You by the hearing of the ear, but now my eye sees You. Therefore I abhor myself, and repent in dust and ashes.* (Job 42:5–6)

Once we get even a small glimpse of Him, everything changes. When He becomes a little clearer in our eyes, our true state becomes clearer as well. That really is revival. It's when we begin to see Him as He is and our neediness and weaknesses are exposed in light of His wonder and greatness.

Corey: In your first season of seeking God for revival, you will hit a wall. This wall causes a bit of disillusionment as your ideas and fantasies of what you thought it would be like are burned up. You may find that you feel further from God than before and that you are more in touch with your weakness than ever before. This is your doorway into a living encounter with Him. It's here you discover He is your reward—not revival or the promises, but Him. It's here that you discover He is beautiful and worthy of your love and sacrifice. Knowing who He is becomes your reward.

I experienced this firsthand right after my initial season of salvation and seeing God move in our hometown. After about six months, I began to see our church go back to business as usual, and it made me so afraid that we were going to lose the spirit of revival. I would get up week after week and yell at everyone to come to the weekly prayer meetings only to find less and less people coming. This made me angrier and angrier, and I began to experience a measure of burnout over my inability to make revival happen.

I felt the Lord tell me in that season to go home and begin to connect with Him at a deeper personal level because He told me, "Revival begins with a breakthrough within." The Lord drew me to some of the early mystics of the Church and their writings. What I read and what the Lord did in my heart gave me a vision for a deeper life of union and intimacy with the indwelling Spirit. It was here He taught me that the secret of Christianity isn't trying harder, but it's looking at Him more and communing with Him more.

Billy: It's what Paul said in Second Corinthians 3:18.

*But we all, with unveiled face, beholding as in a
mirror the glory of the Lord, are being transformed
into the same image from glory to glory, just as by
the Spirit of the Lord.*

Do you have a problem with pride? Stare at Jesus because
He doesn't. Every time I find myself heading back into pride,
which is a little too regularly, I look back at Jesus and am convicted. That conviction leads me to repentance, "Lord, I am
so sorry." Seeing Him humbles me, and it doesn't mean I only
have to ask His forgiveness, but it means I have to repent
to others because there usually are others whom I have hurt
because of my pride.

Corey: The Father has one agenda, and that is to conform
you into the image of His Son. There will only be one kind of
bride at the end of the age, and she will be a leaning, tender,
humble Bride. It's this reality that attracts Heaven and attracts
God because it's who He is and what He's like. It's humility
that becomes the wineskin for revival, and humility will be
entrusted with hosting revival.

[Handwritten margin notes: "but how do you get rid of it?"; " I know I am flesh and will always battle w/ pride. But how do I change?"; "humility is the wineskin for revival."]*

12

HUNGER NECESSARY

Poverty of spirit isn't the only virtue that catches God's eye. Isaiah 57:15 touches on three things that get His attention: humility, hunger, and holiness. Hunger is the second virtue as it only follows that, if you're prideful, you won't acknowledge hunger. Humility must be present in the life of someone before he or she can say, "I'm hungry. Can you help me?"

In this chapter, we want to look at the necessity of hunger and the role it plays in sparking revival and even hosting it.

Billy: When I first began in ministry, I knew I wasn't another T.D. Jakes. I realized I wasn't the best preacher. I just wasn't that guy. I had a friend who was an amazing preacher. He would preach like a house on fire. He was also a dancing machine and could sing like Michael Bolton. And then, sometimes, his messages would be thirty minutes of funny jokes, and everyone would be laughing and entertained by him. And he could turn it on a dime, and the next thing you knew everyone was weeping and travailing under the conviction of the Holy Spirit. I mean, he could do it all and do it well.

Whenever I watched him, I remember thinking, *If I have to be that, I may as well quit ministry right now because I can't.* I also remember during that time encountering passages of Scripture in Psalm 63, Psalm 42, and especially Matthew 5:6, which says, *"Blessed are those who hunger and thirst for righteousness, for they shall be filled."* And then the light went on for me: Hunger doesn't require giftedness. I don't have to be the all-in-one singing, dancing, preaching machine. I don't even have to be able to talk. To be hungry, all I have to do is desire. I could do desire. I already had an appetite on board. If hunger was the necessary requirement to see God's infilling happen, I could hunger.

Psalm 42:2 and Psalm 63:1 both speak of thirsting for God, so when I realized I had a desire resident within me for something "other," something more or greater than myself, I figured I could stir that hunger and feed that desire. My giftedness was not required, but hunger was essential.

I know it is the same for so many of you who are reading right now. You may not be the most gifted person, but that doesn't have to stop you from experiencing an amazing inbreaking of God's glory. He doesn't promise to pour Himself on the most gifted. He promises to pour Himself on the most hungry and thirsty (see Isa. 44:3).

What's interesting with the Lord is He is the only One who can satisfy. He is the greatest addiction there is. How do I know this? Because the more I got of Him, the more I hungered for Him. The more I drank from His wells of salvation, the thirstier I grew for more of His life-giving water. I don't have a great singing voice, and I can't dance. I'm not able to do those things, but I can present myself to Him and hunger for Him.

I remember reading about Kathryn Kuhlman, a healing evangelist during the 1970s. She had a failed marriage. She wasn't very pretty by most standards. She didn't necessarily have a great speaking gift. But she did something that made all the difference: She hungered for God in a profound way. She said,

> I was born without talent....One day I said, "Wonderful Jesus, I don't have a thing. But if you can take nothing and use it, here's nothing. I offer you nothing. I know I love you. All I can give you is my love. I'll give you every ounce of strength in my body."[1]

Her testimony deeply touched me. All she did was offer herself to God and acknowledge He was the only thing she desired. The power of God was released in her life. A captivating anointing came upon her, and her connection with the Holy Spirit was evident in her meetings. People testified that they could hear the sounds of lightning crackling out of her as she prayed for healing. The power of God released through this woman came from her hunger and desire for God.

Beloved, as we said in the opening of this book, we get one go-round in this life. We get one life to live where we're behind the veil in that we don't see God. This is the only opportunity that we will ever have to yearn for Him, to put our desire for Him on display. I don't want to waste this life hungering for stupid stuff that's not going to amount to anything, that's not going to produce anything in my inner man, or that's not going to release something of eternal value. I want to hunger for Him to see His invasion on the earth in my day.

Corey: Jesus simply did things for hungry people that He didn't do for others. Whether it was the Syrophoenician woman of Matthew 15, or blind Bartimaeus in Mark 10, or the woman with the issue of blood in Luke 8, we see time and time again that hungry, desperate people pulled things out of Jesus that no one else did. It's because hunger moves God. Hunger isn't something you make happen, but it is the awareness of your need—the revelation of your need. When spiritual hunger touches you, it's God revealing to you how much you need Him.

The Syrophoenician woman of Matthew 15 had to press past three denials of Jesus to receive her breakthrough. She was an unoffendable woman who refused to be denied. She even took Jesus' offensive statement of saying, *"It is not good to take the children's bread and throw it to the little dogs,"* and she turned it into intercession (Matt. 15:27). This is the nature of hunger. It refuses to be denied.

Bartimaeus had to press past everyone telling him to be quiet and calm down, yet the Bible says, *"But he cried out all the more"* (Mark 10:48). Friend, how many times do you let the

Christian culture you live in dictate your hunger and passion for God and for breakthrough? This blind man refused to let his culture dictate his passion, and he literally stopped the Son of God in His tracks and received healing.

The woman with the issue of blood pressed through the crowd and physically pulled virtue out of Jesus. With all the other healings, we witnessed Jesus initiating the healing, but in this story, she initiated it and pulled it out of Him.

This is what hunger looks like. It's desperate awareness of how much you need God.

I'll never forget a message that I read by John G. Lake on spiritual hunger. This man who shook Africa with the gospel said that the greatest gift he could give to anyone would be hunger. Here is the thing about hunger—you always are grateful yet never satisfied. One of the stories that absolutely wrecked me was Lake's baptism in the Holy Spirit. For years, Lake had experienced a measure of the Holy Spirit's intimacy and power through a dynamic healing ministry, yet he knew there was more. Though everyone around him told him to calm down, he knew there was more. The exact phrase from him that provoked me deeply was, "I felt myself on the borderland of a great spiritual realm, but was unable to enter in fully, so my nature was not satisfied with the attainment."[2]

It was shortly after this that Lake had a life-altering encounter with the Holy Spirit, where he said that he felt his soul and the soul of Jesus Christ become one. The love of God that flowed in him and through him absolutely wrecked him for anything else.

You must understand that there is an internal longing inside you. God put that in you. And living with a raw, violent, aggressive, desperate search is not human zeal. It's not emotionalism. It's a work of God in the soul. It's a gift of God. It may be loud and expressive. It may be very quiet. It's not about what it looks like. It's about a deep gnawing, about a hunger inside that possesses you.

Over the years, I've found that the deeper and longer my prayer life has gone, the shorter and deeper my prayers are becoming.

Pray to get hungry and then pray to sustain it. Go after Philippians 3:12–14, where Paul said:

> *Not that I have already attained, or am already perfected; but I press on, that I may lay hold of that for which Christ Jesus has also laid hold of me. Brethren, I do not count myself to have apprehended; but one thing I do, forgetting those things which are behind and reaching forward to those things which are ahead, I press toward the goal for the prize of the upward call of God in Christ Jesus.*

I see many people who get hungry for God for about a year. They will push and go for God, but the subtle and seductive nature of the heart lures them away from what they were doing, especially if they have received some increased measure of God. They get that, and then it becomes a distant memory instead of fuel to their hunger.

You can't live on the residuals of the past seasons. I've asked God continually to keep me in the old gym in my early days, doing the stuff I did at the beginning, and never letting me graduate from that. Going back looks like more time in prayer and the Word mingled with fasting. Fasting makes you hungry. Fasting makes you raw. It delivers you from the political spirit, the networking spirit, the man-pleasing spirit, and the marketing spirit. Fasting awakens the primal cry for God alone.

Billy: One thing that concerns me is that, as a minister, you can get soft, you know? You can develop your fifteen or twenty messages that you can drop anywhere. People get ministered to, but you can tell when you're not coming out of the overflow of God. Maybe others won't be able to tell, but you will. You know when you're not living close to Him, when you're not hungering for Him. The only way to get yourself out of that rut is to repent for going through the motions and ask the Lord to renew hunger on the inside. And when you begin to hunger again, the hunger will continue to breed more hunger. You must allow God to create a deeper well of hunger, a deeper desire.

So, it's like this. You start off by seeking God. You show up every day and lean in. You ask Him to make you hungry. After a few days, you begin to realize your desire to be with Him has increased. And you notice your revelation of who God is has increased a little more. Every bit that you gain, the grander He becomes to you, and what happens is, if you'll pursue Him, the gap between what you thought you knew and what you actually possess widens, and the hunger increases. In other words, you gain more hunger as you attain more of Him. The only way, therefore, to feed that is by continuing to show up and pursue Him.

There is more of God than you have attained. You may have been marked ten, fifteen, or twenty years ago by a visitation of Him or a vision of what He wanted to release in your life, but then life became difficult. Perhaps you had a measure of attainment, and then what did you do? You pulled back when it got too hard or you felt it would cost too much. I want to tell you that I know the pain of all these choices all too well. And at the same time, I want you to know that those days are not gone from the heart of God. He is inviting you back into them. Allow those old seasons of visitation to stoke that flame inside you again. Let them bring you into that place of desire and spiritual hunger.

Corey: You can have as much of God as you want. Fasting and prayer are not about earning; they're about honoring. I say it this way: Fasting makes me vulnerable to what I've already been brought into so that I can walk into it, experience it, and encounter it.

Fasting weakens your resistance to truth so that the Word of God goes from a tapping hammer to a sledgehammer. Fasting increases your interior capacity to receive and love God. Fasting puts a bull's-eye on your chest and positions you to receive everything from God. Fasting makes you tender and vulnerable to God in a way you've never been before.

Fasting isn't the goal. Intimacy with Him is the goal.

When you fall in love, you rearrange everything. Your time and money belong to the one you love. That's what happens when you touch love. We do it in all our relationships that are important to us. I hear people say, "I just kind of wait to schedule my time with God." Tell your wife that, and you won't have a date night for six months!

We prioritize what we value. We put up boundaries and barriers to keep what we think is important. We give real definition to things. Why? To cultivate intimacy, to grow in knowing and being known, and to create a safe place to go. We do that everywhere and with everyone except God.

I just want you to know it's about God and intimacy with Him. I'm going to be there with Him each morning. I'm going to skip some meals next week—not because I have to or because He's telling me to, but because I love Him. I want to tell Him, "Jesus, You're my first thing. You're my everything." I want a fresh reach inside me. I want fresh tears.

I think there is an element of revival praying that will begin to peak as you grow in intimacy with God. The tears will flow, and travail of the Spirit will come as you cultivate greater intimacy with Him.

Billy: What are the desires you have inside you? I'm not talking about the desire for things or platforms or your social media sphere. What are the desires for God that you have? What are the things you've dreamed of in God?

Have you attained them? Have you seen them realized? Because if you haven't, this is your invitation from God because He's the one who created those dreams inside you. Your flesh didn't come up with them. The fact you have those dreams are His invitation for you to pursue them, and if you touch that just a little bit, hunger will begin to emerge and awaken once again in your soul. And when you begin to hunger, feed your hunger with pursuit. If you seek Him, you will find Him when you seek Him with all your heart (see Deut. 4:29).

NOTES

1. Dr. Margaret English de Alminana, *Kathryn Kuhlman, A Theology of Miracles: Understanding Spiritual Encounter* (Newberry, FL: Bridge-Logos, 2021), chapter 9.

2. John G. Lake, *John G. Lake—Apostle to Africa*, compiled by Gordon Lindsay (Dallas, TX: Christ for the Nations, 1981) 16.

13

HOLINESS ESSENTIAL

Humility and hunger are critical to preparing a person as well as a corporate people to see a spirit of revival released in their midst, but there is another word starting with "h" that in many circles today is seen as an outdated or religious word, and that word is holiness. We must understand that it's not about "earning" revival by these things, but "honoring" revival because we understand that, when God comes, whatever is not like Him will be exposed and ultimately destroyed by the weight of His glory.

Corey: I saw this take place in my first season of walking with the Lord. For about six months in 1997, we saw a move of God hit our small town, and it changed everything. I watched half of the high school either become born again or restored to a new intimacy with God. We had five meetings a week for many months as God shook a small church with His glory. In the aftermath of that season, I watched many things come to light in the leadership team, more specifically, the pastor. He was a leader who had pastored for decades. He had an amazing family and was an example of godliness in our small town, but he began to withdraw himself from the church. In the aftermath of the season of revival, many things began to come to light about him, and that same leader completely left his family and the ministry. I share this story with trembling in my heart because this is the sad reality of what happens in seasons of revival. Everything is exposed.

We all love and long for the Acts 2 outpouring of the Spirit, but it's in these seasons when lies like the ones told by Ananias and Sapphira are revealed. And in their case, their lying to the Holy Spirit led to their deaths. Why so intense? It's because God is close, and God is who He is, and we must prepare for His arrival.

Holiness in the people of God is one of the requirements for hosting His glory in an intensified measure. Holiness is about clean hands, clean hearts, clean mouths, and clean ears. A life of holiness involves everything we look at, listen to, talk about, and do. The preparatory work of the Spirit is to purify His people and get them ready for the Lord's arrival. Many revivalists share the invasive work of the Spirit to cleanse motives and actions in a deep way to prepare for His work in their midst.

Remember two of the conditions that Evan Roberts, the leader of the Welsh revival, said were necessary in preparing for revival:

1. Confess and repent of all sin.
2. Remove any questionable thing in your life.

I believe there are many doubtful or permissible things that God has been putting His finger on in our lives for a while. We have rationalized them or justified them or made excuses for them, and God is requiring us to fully remove them from our lives. Holiness is when God prepares us for capability with Him. God's holiness is His superior beauty and splendor and majesty that separate Him from everything common and created. His holiness is His separation, and this is His gift to His people who hunger for Him.

Peter calls us to be holy because God is holy, which means as we behold God's holiness in Scripture, He transforms us from within to love the things He loves and to hate the things He hates (see 1 Pet. 15–16).

Billy: We want to revisit Isaiah's prophecy,

> *For thus says the High and Lofty One who inhabits eternity, whose name is Holy: "I dwell in the high and holy place, with him who has a contrite and humble spirit, to revive the spirit of the humble, and to revive the heart of the contrite ones."* (Isaiah 57:15)

Something that has long troubled me is that, when I was a young man, I had the opportunity to be in meetings with ministers who moved in the power of God with preaching, salvations, and miracles, and then when I talked to them behind the scenes, they told carnal stories and off-color jokes. There were times I was heartbroken to find that the men I had received so much from weren't in private what they appeared to be in public. I don't say these things with judgment in my heart, but with a brokenness and a mourning, knowing that there is so much more to living and loving Jesus than putting forward a face publicly that isn't reality privately.

I puzzled over the inequity, "If this is the case with the preachers, what about the people? Do we just keep going and act like everything is fine? Do we turn a blind eye to hypocrisy because people are getting 'blessed' in meetings? Is this how it's supposed to be?" From the deepest place in my being, I said, *"No!"* I want the real thing no matter the cost. I want to know the real Jesus and express His real nature regardless of who follows. I want Him to make me so sick at the smell of pretense that I never want to touch it. I'm not imagining that I've arrived, but I am freshly surrendering myself to Him so He can conform me to His dream.

Holiness is born from a craving for reality. If we want the real Jesus, we will turn loose every other thing.

I haven't always been this way. I've lived seasons where my public persona overshadowed my personal holiness. God has taken me through deep moments of conviction, where He has placed His hand upon me and wouldn't let me continue with my charade until I repented both personally and publicly of my sin. David described the Lord's burning conviction this way,

For day and night Your hand was heavy upon me;
my vitality was turned into the drought of summer.
Selah. I acknowledged my sin to You, and my iniq-
uity I have not hidden. I said, "I will confess my
transgressions to the Lord," and You forgave the
iniquity of my sin. (Psalm 32:4–5)

Even recently, He pierced my heart, burning me down with the fire of His conviction until I was in ashes confessing my sin.

Corey: I well know the gap between my external reputation and my personal holiness in God. I've known boredom, disappointment, and pain that have caused me to let down some of my guard over what I watch, what I listen to, or how I speak. I've experienced the spirit of conviction striking my heart and calling me back to original vows before God. I've known the wrestling over the permissible but not beneficial things in my life that He required of me. I know the times I've resisted Him, and I know the times of bowing low and returning to Him.

Billy: I believe He is going to release this most precious gift of conviction to the Church once again, where we are crushed into powder under the weight of our broken ways so that we cry out to Him, the only One who saves. It's in this crucible that purity is born. It's in this crushing that holiness breaks our distractions. Oh, how we need His purging fire to consume every part of us until only He remains, until we are wholly His. We need to become comfortable with the beauty of repentance.

David's cry in Psalm 12:1 is resounding in my ears and heart, *"Help, Lord, for the godly man ceases! For the faithful disappear from among the sons of men."* This lament strikes a chord in my depths. What will become of this generation when the godly leaders we have followed have passed on? Will the Lord find another generation that give themselves to the ancient paths of holiness, humility, and spiritual hunger as the former generation did? Or will we be left with a church following leaders who have learned to work the crowd but haven't rent their hearts?

When I think of my own generation, I tremble at the thought that the fathers we have followed are entering their twilight. Will there be another generation of Lou Engles and Mike Bickles who will lead us into brokenness, holiness, fasting, and prayer?

Corey: The deception that so easily creeps in for leaders is when we see our gifting or platform as our secret relationship with God. I'm so desperate to see a new generation of leaders arise who are as humble, hungry, and holy in secret as they are in public. I long to see the fear of the Lord touch worship leaders in these days where there is no difference between their bedrooms and prayer rooms.

Mike Bickle, a spiritual father of ours, would always use the phrase, "happy holiness." What he meant by this statement was that the pursuit of holiness is not the begrudging gritting of the teeth as we say *no* to the bad things, but it is a life that is absolutely intoxicated by God. I believe that God is raising up end-time revivalists who will be so happy in Him that they won't sell that for anything in the world.

Jesus Himself is anointed with the oil of gladness because of His love for righteousness and hatred of wickedness.

> *You love righteousness and hate wickedness; there-*
> *fore God, Your God, has anointed You with the oil of*
> *gladness more than Your companions.* (Psalm 45:7)

I believe that we are going to see a new generation of leaders who will not compromise as the glory of God begins to increase because their lives of holiness aren't just outward behaviors but are manifestations of a deep fascination and pleasure in God and His beauty.

It's not only the pleasure of His holiness that is marking us, but it's His fire. I keep hearing the phrase, "blazing holiness." It is coming back to the Church! The baptism of fire is coming to those who hunger for revival, and the fire will consume everything that is not like God.

Billy: I have found that the greater the public persona someone has, the harder it is for them to stay pure. I'm convinced the days of celebrity Christianity are over. I'm convinced that the Lord is purifying the "sons of Levi" with an unquenchable fire. As Jesus said, *"His winnowing fan is in His hand, and He will thoroughly clean out His threshing floor, and gather His wheat into the barn; but He will burn up the chaff with unquenchable fire"* (Matt. 3:12). Jesus isn't going to continue to allow compromise to exist in His leaders or in His Church. He is calling us to a purity and a holiness that come from deep intimacy and closeness.

The Lord is judging our compromises right now. He is judging all our false allegiances. He is calling the Church out of loyalty to everything else but Himself so that He can have a people who are wholly His own. He is not content to share us with another.

And why? Why would God want to judge us this way? Because He wants to *dwell* in our midst. He is not satisfied with momentary encounters anymore. He doesn't want to simply visit our assemblies for moments of power. He wants to be the glory dwelling among us. He wants to come and remain. And He can't do that among a people in compromise with leaders in compromise. Isaiah knew this, so he said, *"Woe is me, for I am undone! Because I am a man of unclean lips, and I dwell in the midst of a people of unclean lips"* (Isa. 6:5). He knew, for God to come and dwell, the people would have to turn from their sin and be cleansed. It is the same with us. If we are ever to see God dwelling among us in glory and habitation, we must get rid of the compromise in our lives.

Holiness isn't about walking around with a sour look and a judgmental attitude. Holiness is about the longing deep inside to be with Him. When we begin to allow that ache to mount in our souls, we are brought to a reckoning: Do we want Him more than anything else? Is there something in the way between us and Him? Our longing for Him to come compels us to rid ourselves of all that stands in the way. Holiness isn't born out of duty; it's born out of desire.

If we're going to see revival, it's going to come with conviction, repentance, purity, and holiness. There is no revival without holiness. I heard a revival preacher say this a long time ago, it may sound a little cheesy, but it's just true, "If there's one thing I know about the Holy Spirit, it's His f.... name, Holy."

We can't imagine that we are going to see the fullness of God's glory without holiness burning in and upon our hearts. It's my heart's cry, and I pray it's yours as well. *Make me like You, Jesus. Burn away everything that's in the way. Cleanse me and purify me until I'm a dwelling place where You can rest.*

Corey: Holiness is more than the outward actions, but it is the manifestation of inward springs from which our actions flow. Holiness is when God reorients you to the surpassing greatness of His beauty and where you drink deeply of the river of His pleasures. Holiness is when you find your supreme joy in Him and in pleasing Him.

Let's ask God right now to baptize us afresh in the fire of the Holy Spirit and that His blazing holiness would mark us deeply.

> *Jesus, we want to love what You love and hate what You hate. We ask You to make us like You so that we can be closer to You and that You can fully be Yourself in our lives and in our midst. We long for You to come and dwell among us. Get us ready for revival by baptizing us in the Holy Spirit and fire. Consume everything in our lives that is not of You and that will not stand when You come. We ask You to consume every bit of pride, arrogance, independence, lust, envy, competition, and comparison in our lives. Please have mercy on us and confront every place, person, and thing that*

we run to for comfort that is not of You.

We cry out that You will get us ready by purifying us from within and that we would truly find You more beautiful, pleasurable, and fascinating than anything that this world has to offer. May You and Your Word be our number-one source of joy, peace, and comfort.

Holy Spirit, come now and consume us completely. We welcome You and invite You to have Your way in our lives. Baptize this whole generation in the blazing holiness of Your love.

Make us holy as You are Holy. In Jesus' name. Amen.

14

RECLAIMING REVIVAL

We're longing for something real. We hope this truth has hit your heart as you've read these pages. We want God's revival and nothing less. We want the real thing. We won't rest until we see God move in a way that leaves no doubt that it's Him. We've asked the Lord to use this book to strike and mark hearts with the same branding that we both carry. And as we wrap up, we want to make sure that what we're aiming for is nothing less than what only Heaven can offer.

We believe an entire generation is waiting for a sound that calls them to awakening. Our prayer is that you've heard something of that sound in these pages. As the deep inside us resonates with the deep inside you, we want to access the deep places in the heart of God for Heaven to come down.

We believe we're at a crossroads in our nation. The time clock of the earth is ticking down to the last minutes. We're coming to a moment where it's literally revival or we die. And because the hour is urgent, we must have a definitive vision of what we're all seeking so that we can contend together for literal days of Heaven on Earth.

Corey: Billy and I wrote this book because we are gripped with a vision to see true revival break into our nation and the nations of the earth. We've both tasted a measure of the move of God but are not satisfied over what we have seen. We are truly grateful for every time anyone is touched by God at any time in any setting. We especially never get used to seeing God touch someone for the first time as they cry fresh tears from encountering His love. We love every time God moves in a meeting or at a conference and touches His people, but this is not revival. We love every healing and deliverance, but this is not revival. We love every word of knowledge and prophetic utterance, but this is not revival.

We've done a great disservice to this generation and future generations by calling everything *revival*. When we make everything revival, then nothing is revival.

Billy: Man, I love that. I think many of us, in our hunger for revival, have called almost everything from church growth to good meetings *revival*, and it's because we have never seen the real thing. In our zeal, we have dumbed down the truth of revival. We can't lose the apostolic or historic picture of what revival really is, and we can't allow our own barrenness to redefine revival in terms that are completely inferior to the reality.

Corey: We need to reclaim this word in our day, and we do this by reconnecting to what biblical and historical revival looks like. As we have seen, the book of Acts gives us snapshots of what revival looks like: supernatural invasions of the Holy Spirit that release preaching that simultaneously cuts thousands of hearts who cry out, "What must we do to be saved?"

I just want to take a moment and in a raw way do our best to paint the picture once again.

Revival is when people hear sounds of a mighty rushing wind and see divided tongues of fire.

Revival is when buildings where prayer meetings are being held begin to shake under the power of God.

Revival is when people lie to the Holy Spirit about the proceeds that came in from a sale of land and they are immediately struck by God and the fear of God seizes everyone, causing everyone to fear to join the church, yet numbers are added daily.

Billy: Revival is when leaders in the highest offices are crippled under conviction of their own sin and the sin of their nation.

Revival is when whole cities like Ephesus are filled with the tangible fear of the Lord.

Corey: Revival is when whole cities like Samaria are filled with joy as the Word of God goes forth.

Billy: Revival is when lifelong paralytics are miraculously healed, sparking citywide repentance and citywide persecution.

Corey: Revival is when religious terrorists are struck by a blinding light and are saved and turned into apostles.

Billy: Revival is when the Word of God prevails mightily upon an entire region and masses are convicted and converted.

Corey: Revival is when God breaks out in groups of people that are seen as unclean or not worthy and God blows open a door into entirely new people groups.

Billy: Revival is when the salvations, signs, wonders, and miracles in one town are the dinner conversations in the surrounding regions and everyone is drawn to come to see what has happened.

Corey: Revival is when prayer meetings release angels that deliver apostolic leaders from prison and then the king dies that is persecuting the apostolic leaders.

Revival is when the gospel begins to explode like a wildfire throughout regions and no one can stop it—where the smartest, most refined, most educated, and most articulate are confronted with the simplicity and power of the gospel and cities are shaken.

Billy: Revival is when the power brokers in every sphere of society are confronted by the nearness and bigness of God—where the political, entertainment, governmental, and economic sectors all stand at attention because of the shock and intervention of the divine presence.

Corey: Revival is when cities like Thessalonica are turned upside down and every demon in the region is provoked.

Revival is when a handful of believers erupt into 25,000 and a whole idol industry is bankrupted and the Word of God prevails over whole regions. It's when everyone brings all their immoral and idolatrous paraphernalia to the city square and they have public burnings because the spirit of conviction is exposing everything and everyone.

Billy: Those are all accounts from the book of Acts of what revival can look like. What about some of the stories we've heard from history that color in the lines for us?

Corey: Revival is when whole islands come under the manifest spirit of conviction and people begin to turn themselves into the cops because everything they've ever done wrong was made known to them.

Billy: Revival is when throughout a whole region you can see lights on in houses and hear people groaning in travail over their sin and for the salvation of souls at three and four o'clock in the morning.

Corey: Revival is when buildings are visible to the naked eye as burning and on fire.

Revival is when the glory cloud fills the room and limbs grow back, eyes are restored, and the deaf hear.

Billy: Revival is when racial barriers are destroyed and the color lines are washed away by the blood of Jesus. When Black, White, Asian, and Hispanic are all one in Jesus.

Revival is when the news of God's habitation doesn't need media to promote it because the word is heralded abroad that God has come down and the sound resonates with the ache of eternity in the hearts of men.

Corey: Revival is when God comes close and Heaven bears down on Earth—when eternity bears down on time and people forget to eat, drink, or sleep.

Billy: Revival changes everything. It changes the way we see and understand God. It changes the way we love and serve one another. And in revival, God changes how He relates to us. He no longer restrains Himself, but instead He moves with force and intention that upend our world. The most rooted strongholds are uprooted, and the most established rituals are overturned.

Revival disrupts the normal course of religious affairs, it suspends the normal programming of human lives, and it radically accelerates the progress of the Kingdom.

In revival, God draws near, and nothing else matters.

Corey: This is what is in our hearts and what we long to see restored in our generation. Both of us are so tired of hype and exaggeration. We are so tired of all the marketing gimmicks that state one thing is happening when it's not. It's time for a restored vision for revival. When our vision is restored, our faith will be awakened.

Billy: We must get the apostolic vision of what can happen in revival. We must reclaim this most precious word. God promises a recovery of breath to those who pursue Him. We must connect to the depth of that. We can't diminish what life from the dead, what breath to the breathless means for the Church and the world. Oh, that we would see and believe and contend for what is possible—that we would apprehend this high and precious gift of Heaven once again.

> *Revival and nothing less. Revival or we never rest.*
> *Revival now, oh God, we cry. Revival now or we*
> *will die!*

ABOUT COREY RUSSELL

Corey Russell's passion is to awaken the Church across the earth to the beauty of Jesus, intimacy with the Holy Spirit, and the power of prayer. He has written six books and released five prayer albums. He and his family spent 18 years in Kansas City, Missouri, with International House of Prayer, and he is currently on the staff of Global Upper Room based in Dallas, Texas. He has been married to his wife, Dana, for over 20 years and has three daughters and one son.

ABOUT BILLY HUMPHREY

Billy Humphrey is the director of GateCity Church, where 24/7, live worship and prayer has continued ceaselessly since 2006. From the place of night-and-day worship and prayer, the gospel goes forth across the city of Atlanta, even to the ends of the earth. Billy is the author of three books, *The Culture of the Kingdom*, *Unceasing*, and *To Know Him*. He has been married to his wife, Maribeth, for over 25 years and has three sons and one daughter.

YOUR
Prophetic
COMMUNITY

Are you passionate about hearing God's voice, walking with Jesus, and experiencing the power of the Holy Spirit?

Destiny Image is a community of believers with a passion for equipping and encouraging you to live the prophetic, supernatural life you were created for!

We offer a fresh helping of practical articles, dynamic podcasts, and powerful videos from respected, Spirit-empowered, Christian leaders to fuel the holy fire within you.

Sign up now to get awesome content delivered to your inbox
destinyimage.com/sign-up

 Destiny Image